PRETTY QUILLED CARDS

25+ CREATIVE DESIGNS FOR GREETINGS & CELEBRATIONS

Cecelia Louie

LARK

LARK

An Imprint of Sterling Publishing
387 Park Avenue South
New York, NY 10016

ISBN 978-1-4547-0784-4

Library of Congress Cataloging-in-Publication Data

Louie, Cecelia.
   Pretty quilled cards : 25+ creative designs for greetings & celebrations / Cecelia Louie.
      pages cm
   Includes bibliographical references and index.
   ISBN 978-1-4547-0784-4 (alkaline paper)
   1. Greeting cards. 2. Paper flowers. 3. Paper quillwork. I. Title.
   TT872.L68 2014
   745.594'1--dc23
                                   2013028310

ISBN 978-1-4547-0784-4

Distributed in Canada by Sterling Publishing
c/o Canadian Manda Group, 165 Dufferin Street
Toronto, Ontario, Canada M6K 3H6
Distributed in the United Kingdom by GMC Distribution Services
Castle Place, 166 High Street, Lewes, East Sussex, England BN7 1XU
Distributed in Australia by Capricorn Link (Australia) Pty. Ltd.
P.O. Box 704, Windsor, NSW 2756, Australia

For information about custom editions, special sales, and premium and corporate purchases,
please contact Sterling Special Sales at 800-805-5489 or specialsales@sterlingpublishing.com.

Email academic@larkbooks.com for information about desk and examination copies.
The complete policy can be found at larkcrafts.com.

Every effort has been made to ensure that all the information in this book is accurate. However, due to
differing conditions, tools, and individual skills, the publisher cannot be responsible for any injuries, losses,
and other damages that may result from the use of the information in this book.

Manufactured in China

2 4 6 8 10 9 7 5 3 1

larkcrafts.com

Contents

Introduction

When I saw my first example of quilling in the library, my eyes would not stop following the spiraling curves. It seemed to be a complicated art form, but I soon realized how easy and inexpensive it is. Ever since, I have enjoyed creating countless customized gifts for friends and family.

Quilling (paper filigree) is an art form that has been passed on from the Renaissance. Once made with gilded strips and feather quills, the arrangements decorated book covers and religious items. Today, pre-cut paper is wound around a quilling tool, shaped, and glued to create a myriad of expressive pieces.

Experienced quillers will notice that my style is a bit unorthodox, perhaps a little looser than you might be used to seeing. I love the exaggerated spirals and dynamic look I can create by working this way. I hope you'll enjoy my unique style, too.

When I'm teaching others how to quill, they often say, "I didn't know it was so easy!" Then I love watching the fever take them up and away, as they dream about what they'll quill next.

Happy quilling to you!

Cecelia Louie

Quilling Basics

After borrowing a few basic supplies from your own craft bins or buying just a handful of inexpensive odds and ends, you'll be set to quill.

SUPPLIES

Paper

A myriad of pre-cut quilling paper colors are available in ¹⁄₁₆-inch (1.6 mm), ⅛-inch (3 mm), ¼-inch (6 mm), ⅜-inch (9.5 mm) and ½-inch (1.3 cm) widths. ⅛-inch is the most commonly used width and is primarily used in this book. For the wider widths used in fringed projects, I have simply cut my own.

Tools

The two types of quilling tools are slotted and needle. A slotted tool has a gap in the middle of a metal rod. Beginner quillers can easily slip their paper in the slot, ensuring the paper will catch and turn around the tool. However, it leaves a crimp in the innermost coil and a larger center hole than the needle tool. A slotted tool is needed when coiling a fringed paper strip.

A needle tool, on the other hand, looks like an elongated pin, and it does not have a slot for holding the end of the paper. The thin taper of the needle tool allows for the tiniest coils without crimping. It takes a bit of practice to use, but I've seen some beginner quillers take to it right from the start. Both tools will need consistent tension when you're coiling your paper.

Additionally, you'll need a few other tools: Both regular and reverse tweezers are invaluable for reaching into tiny areas to squeeze a join or place elements while gluing. You will need a paper crimper for some of the projects in this book. You can make one from toy parts or computer-printer components (search for online tutorials), or you can purchase one from a craft store. Of course you'll want a pencil to mark your paper, and a mechanical one is best for precision. For scoring folds, I use a dried-out ballpoint pen, but if a dry pen is not on hand, I use my needle tool/awl for scoring. Keep the angle low, rather than upright, so the

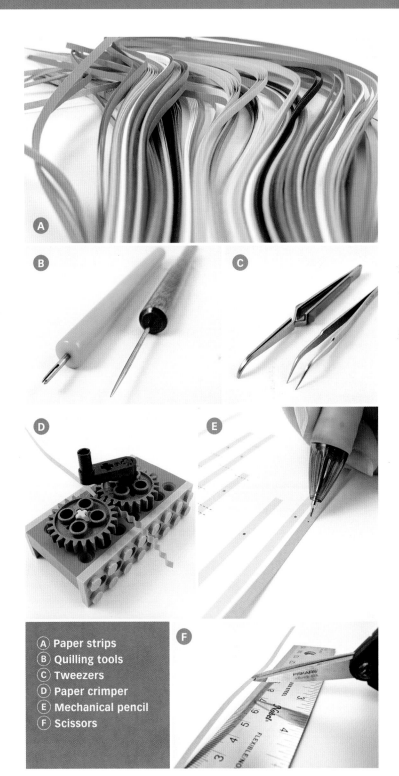

Ⓐ **Paper strips**
Ⓑ **Quilling tools**
Ⓒ **Tweezers**
Ⓓ **Paper crimper**
Ⓔ **Mechanical pencil**
Ⓕ **Scissors**

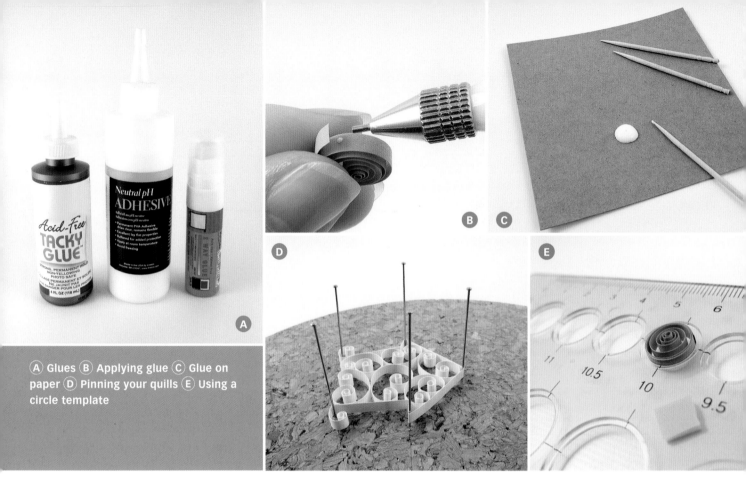

(A) Glues **(B)** Applying glue **(C)** Glue on paper **(D)** Pinning your quills **(E)** Using a circle template

scoring is smooth and not scraping the paper fibers. ⅛- and ¼-inch hole punches are useful for many paper projects, from allowing ribbon to thread through a tag to creating highlights in a gingerbread man's eyes. A ruler with imperial units makes it easy to measure small pieces of paper. Finally, you'll need scissors to cut strips of paper in exact lengths.

Glue

Archival PVA glue dries clear and is thicker than standard glue. That's what you'll want to use when you're certain of how you want things arranged. I occasionally use temporary glue while deciding on a composition and need items to stop fidgeting, and then after I've decided on a permanent layout, I'll dip the item in the PVA glue. For applying the glue, a fine-tipped bottle is best, so that you can get a precise dot of glue.

Scrap cards are useful for holding a puddle of glue to draw from while you work, and toothpicks are great for picking up and dabbing spots of glue. You will make things easier for yourself if you keep a box of tissues nearby for cleaning your fingers and tools, and wiping away excess glue.

Other Supplies

A corkboard wrapped in plastic cling wrap makes a great work surface for pinning items in place as you go. The plastic prevents your paper from getting inadvertently glued to the corkboard along the way. You can also photocopy the templates in this book and slide them under the cling wrap to use as a guide.

You'll also need a circle template, which you can find at a dollar store, an office supply store, or online. When you want a shape of an exact size, coil the strip, release it within a circle template, and allow it to expand. The templates tend to be quite thin, however, and I find my coils will sometimes slip out, so I use adhesive foam squares to raise the circle template to about half the height of my strip so it stays securely "fenced in."

BASIC QUILLING TECHNIQUES

Softening

Softening is a technique you will use a lot. It prepares the paper for quilling so that your coils will appear smoother. It is very simple. To soften, pull the paper between your tool and your finger, as shown in Ⓐ. I generally pre-soften all my strips unless the design calls for a straight edge, because I find the paper is more malleable that way.

Note: I often have to fold a strip to define segments before I soften it. Since softening can flatten out a creased fold, I tend to crease the fold sharply a second time after softening to redefine the crisp fold I had before. This step is a meticulous step that I like to do, but it's completely up to you whether or not you want to do this extra finishing. I will occasionally instruct you to do it, as it is a natural part of my workflow, but if you find it unnecessary, simply skip it.

Scraping

Scraping is a firmer version of softening, similar to curling ribbon for a gift. To scrape, firmly drag the paper against your finger as shown in photo Ⓑ to achieve a tighter curl.

Rubbing

Rubbing sculpts and rounds the paper in specific areas, as you see in photos Ⓒ and Ⓓ. To rub, press the paper against your finger using your tool as shown, and rub from left to right. The paper will curl in this rubbed area.

Crimping

To crimp your quilling paper, just feed the strip between the gears of your crimper (which have teeth), and turn the lever or knob to move the paper through, pressing the paper into a corrugated pattern. When you need a specific length of crimped paper, be sure to crimp and then measure, not the other way around!

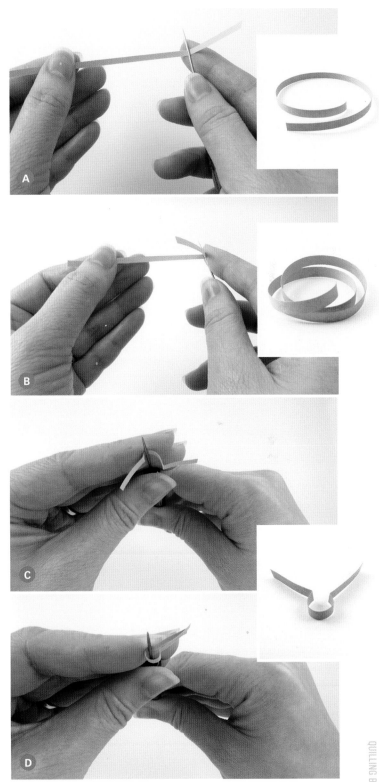

COILS

Making Loose Coils with a Slotted Tool

1. Slip the end of your paper into the slot. Turn the tool either left or right, winding the paper around the tool. (A)

2. Use your fingernail to keep the coils even. Your opposite hand will guide the paper, determine tension, and prevent unraveling. (B)

3. Using the top of your fingernail, push the completed roll off (see photo (C)). Don't pull the roll off, or it may spiral and unravel, as shown in photo. (D)

4. Release the coil, and allow it to relax into a loose scroll. (E)

5. Dab a small amount of glue on the end and press against the roll with tweezers for a few seconds. (F) (G)

6. You've completed your loose coil! (H)

Hint: Using a slotted tool will leave a hole and a kink. To smooth the kink in the innermost coil, slip a toothpick in the center and twirl it around.

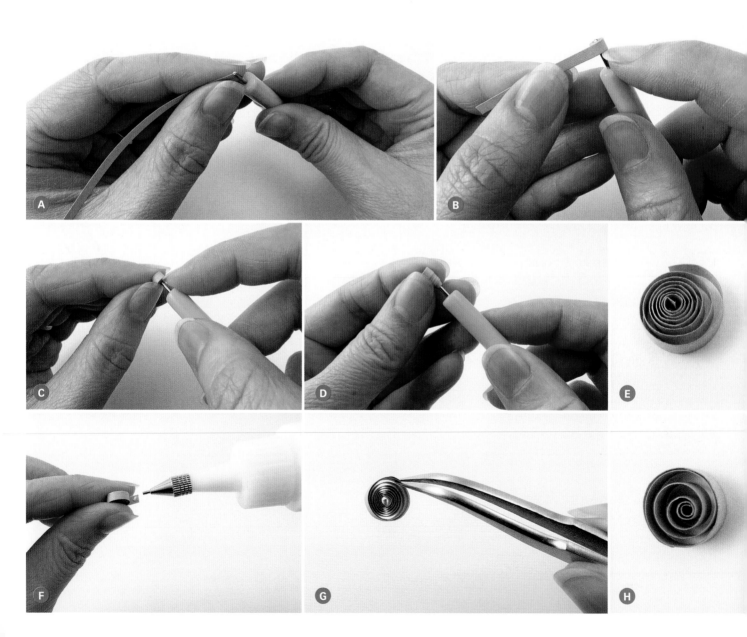

Making Loose Coils with a Needle Tool

1. Set the paper on your index finger and place the needle tool at the very end of it, as shown. Place your thumb on top and press the tool and paper against your index finger. (A)

2. Rub your finger and thumb as if removing glue, catching the paper up so it wraps around the needle tool. If the paper does not catch and coil, lightly moisten your finger and try again.

Wrap the paper around the needle, holding the tool in place, rather than turning the tool. The hand holding the paper will guide the strip, determine tension, and prevent unraveling. The hand holding the tool will keep the coil even by intermittently guiding it with the top of a fingernail. (B)

3. Push the coil off of the top of the tool and let it relax. (C)

4. Now glue your coil together as I described for the slotted tool, and voila! (D)

Note: Needle tools generally create tighter spirals than slotted tools. (E)

Hint: A few of the projects in this book require a specific size of coil (7 mm, for example). Use your circle template as I described on page 6 to get exact sizes.

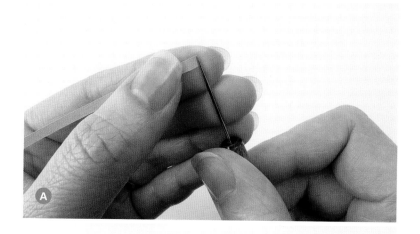

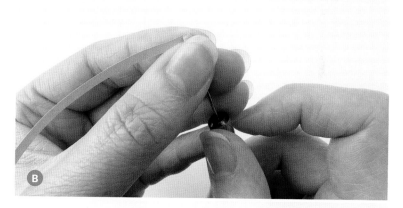

Note on Coils

When a specific size of coil is needed, release your coil (before gluing) within a circle template and allow it to expand. Dab glue at the end, and press the coil against it, as shown.

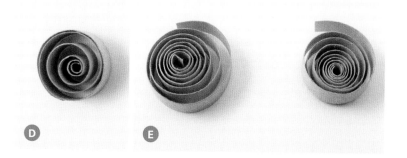

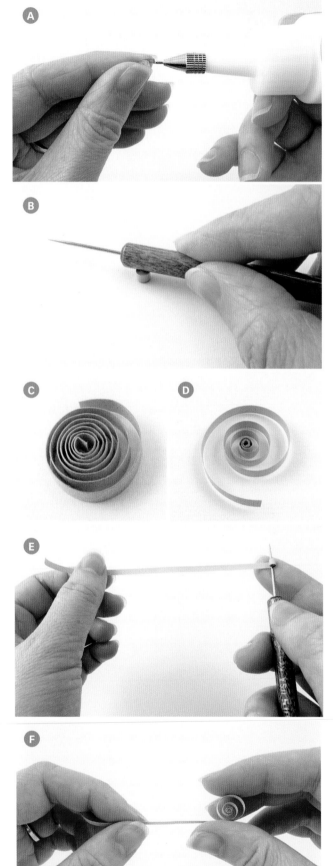

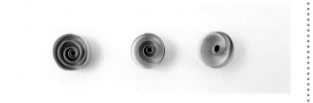

Tight Coils

To make a tight coil, do not release the coil after removing it from the tool. Simply dab glue on the end and press against the roll for a few seconds. Using the top of your fingernail, push the completed roll off the tool. Press the coil against a flat surface to ensure all the coils are even. Ⓐ Ⓑ

SCROLLS

Loose Scrolls

To make a loose scroll, you simply make a coil and don't glue it. A loose scroll is a coil without the glue! Ⓒ

Looser Scrolls

You will often need an even looser scroll (see Ⓓ). To accomplish this:

1. Gently unravel your loose scroll as shown, leaving the few innermost rings alone. Ⓔ

2. Gently re-coil the paper by hand, creating a looser scroll. Ⓕ

This loosening is something I do with almost every coil I make.

C-Scrolls

1. Coil both ends halfway down the length of a paper strip in the same direction, forming a C shape. (A)

2. Gently unravel both ends, leaving the innermost rings. Now you have a very loose C-scroll. (B)

3. Re-coil by hand to make it a little tighter. (C)

S-Scrolls

1. Coil both ends of your paper strip in opposite directions, forming an S shape. (D)

2. Gently unravel, leaving the innermost rings. (E)

3. Re-coil both ends by hand. (F)

The S-scroll can easily be any size you need for the space you have to fill, based on how tightly you re-coil it. Re-coiling one end smaller and the other end larger will result in an asymmetric S-scroll. (G)

Hint: To create a gentle S shape, soften one end, turn the paper around, and soften the other end in the opposite direction. (H)

Question-Mark Scroll

This is a loose interpretation of an S-scroll—more of a question mark, really. So that's what I'll call it throughout the book. (I)

1. Coil one end of your paper strip.

2. Gently unravel it, leaving the innermost rings.

3. Re-coil by hand.

4. Soften the other end in the opposite direction. (J)

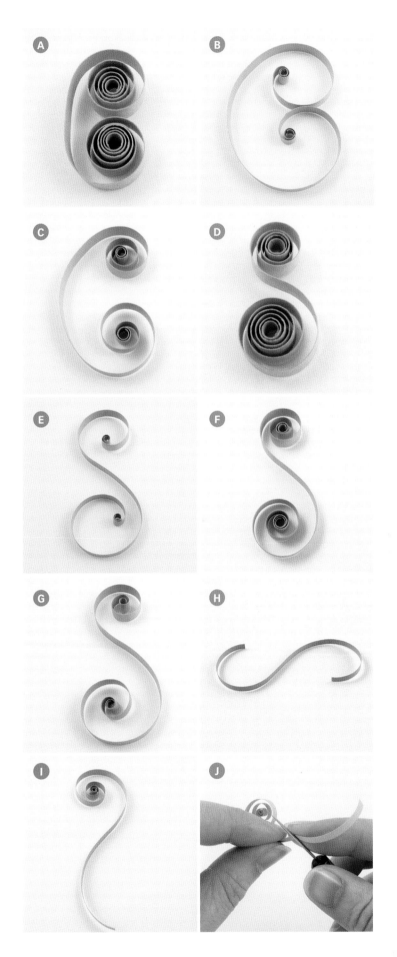

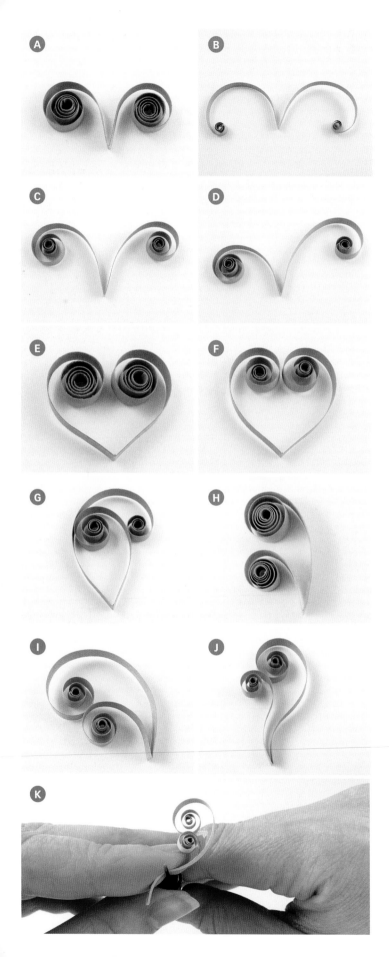

V-Scrolls

1. Fold a paper strip in two equal or unequal halves, and coil both ends outward. (A)

2. Gently uncoil, leaving the innermost rings. (B)

3. Re-coil by hand to create your V-scroll. (C)

4. Re-coiling with different tension will easily create an asymmetric V-scroll. (D)

Heart Scroll

1. Fold a paper strip in two equal or unequal halves, and coil both ends inward. (E)

2. Uncoil and re-coil by hand to create a looser heart scroll. (F)

Allow one coil of your heart scroll to wrap the other to create a tucked heart scroll. (G)

Hint: At any time, the V-scroll can become the heart scroll, and vice versa, simply by inverting the fold.

Same-Sided Scroll

1. Fold a paper strip in two equal or unequal halves, and coil both ends in the same direction. (H)

2. Uncoil and re-coil by hand to create a looser same-sided scroll. (I)

Hint: To stylize the "V" portion of your same-sided scroll, rub near the folded area in the opposite direction. (See page 7 for rubbing instructions.) (J) (K)

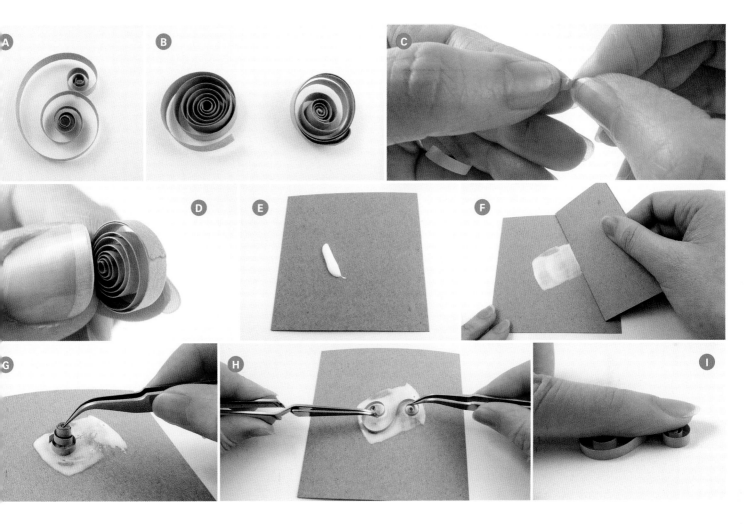

TIPS

Here are a handful of helpful hints—some things I've learned over the years—that will reduce your learning curve:

- I will occasionally ask you to make an *asymmetric* scroll. If you simply wind one end up more than the other one so that end is larger than the other, it gives the scroll a different look. See the example photo of an asymmetric C-scroll. (A)

- Uneven tension and paper guidance can result in uneven coils. Fortunately, paper is forgiving. Simply uncoil your paper and try it again. (B)

- Tearing instead of cutting your paper strips creates a less visible join. (C) (D)

- When you're ready to glue your final piece, smear a puddle of glue to make it shallow, and then press your quilled piece into the puddle to coat the entire edge. The examples shown use a piece of scrap card, but less porous surfaces, such as a plastic yogurt lid work very well, and can be reused for the same purpose after scraping off the dried glue. (E) (F)

- When you're dipping a coil into glue, a tornado can form as you lift it (as shown in (G)), misshaping delicate coils. Here are three ways to make lifting less destructive:

  ‣ decrease the glue puddle depth
  ‣ don't dip the entire coil at once
  ‣ use two tweezers to pick up the quilled piece (H)

- Position your dipped piece over your surface and confirm its placement before gluing it down. Then set it down and use your fingers to gently press all the coils down evenly. (I)

- Facing all the coils in the same direction gives a subtle sense of continuity in your finished piece. (A)

- Empty chocolate boxes and plastic fishing tackle bins have individual compartments—great for storing small bits in progress. (B)

- Dampen a piece of tissue paper and place it in the bottom of a shot glass. Place your glue bottle upside down in the glass so it's always ready to use and doesn't dry out. (C)

ABOUT THIS BOOK

Each project will have a list of project components, like a recipe. I've provided actual-size cutting guides, so all you have to do to get the correct lengths of paper is lay your quilling paper strip on top of the guides and cut where indicated. I have also included a symbols key (below left) so you'll know where to fold, glue, soften, or draw pencil marks.

The project components are alphabetized in order of usage, and they correspond to labeled diagrams. It can be helpful to photocopy each individual diagram and place it on your corkboard under the plastic cling wrap as a tracing guide. This will allow you to pin and glue components without them sticking to your template. Don't fret if your pieces don't match the diagrams exactly, they're just guides. Take pleasure in knowing your quilling is uniquely yours!

The Instructions section of each project shows you how to make each piece in the order in which you will need them, and will refer to photos, illustrations, or other pages for further details.

For some of the projects, I've included accents—background designs and embellishments—that you can copy onto cardstock, and trim to size using a ruler and a craft knife. There are crop mark guides at the four corners of each card template to help you align your ruler so you get a straight cut.

As when you're working with a recipe, nothing here is set in stone. Feel free to change out colors or make other adjustments to fit your aesthetic. My main goals in this book are to demystify quilling for beginners and to show experienced quillers some new tricks. I hope you will find plenty of inspiration in these pages!

Symbols Key

┆ Fold

| Cut

▪ Pencil mark

• Glue

✳ Point of reference (varies with project)

▲ Soften or coil (varies with project)

PROJECTS

· · · · · · · · · · ·

Birthday Cupcakes

SKILLS YOU'LL NEED: • C-scroll (page 11) • S-scroll (page 11) • Rubbing (page 7)
• Loose coil (pages 8-9) • Softening (page 7)

Cupcake with Candle Project Components SKILL LEVEL: ●●○○○

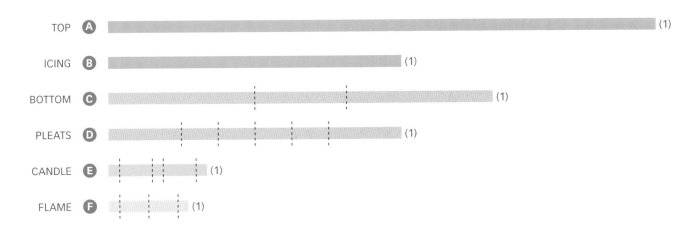

TOP	**A**	(1)
ICING	**B**	(1)
BOTTOM	**C**	(1)
PLEATS	**D**	(1)
CANDLE	**E**	(1)
FLAME	**F**	(1)

Cupcake with Cherry Project Components

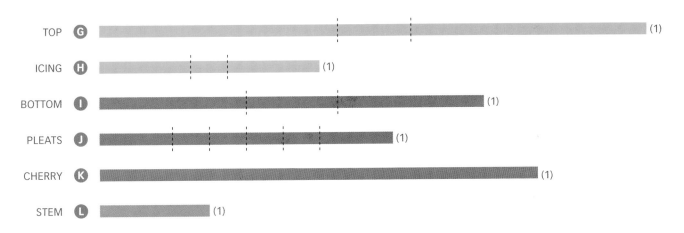

TOP	**G**	(1)
ICING	**H**	(1)
BOTTOM	**I**	(1)
PLEATS	**J**	(1)
CHERRY	**K**	(1)
STEM	**L**	(1)

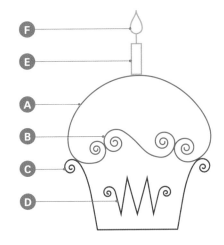

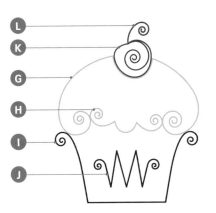

Step 1

Step 2

Step 3

Step 4

Step 5

Step 6

1. TOP

Create a C-scroll using strip (A).

2. ICING

Create an S-scroll using strip (B).

3. BOTTOM

Crease the folds and scroll the ends of strip (C) outward to form the bottom part of the cupcake.

4. PLEATS

Zig-zag fold strip (D) along the dotted lines, and then coil the ends outward as shown. To achieve tight creases, use tweezers to compress the folds as shown in the photo at left.

5. CANDLE

Fold strip (E) into a rectangle along the dotted lines indicated on the guide, and glue the overlap closed.

6. FLAME

Fold strip (F) where indicated, and then rub the curves in to shape the flame. Glue the wick together to complete the flame.

7. ASSEMBLY

Photocopy the cake stand template on page 21 at 100% onto white cardstock and trim at the crop marks. Glue the bottom of the cupcake onto it (using a ruler as a straight edge if needed). Glue the top in place next, securing one end first and then the other, so that both ends touch the top of the bottom piece.

Place the icing strip inside the C-scroll that forms the top, and adjust the size if necessary before gluing it in place. Glue the pleats inside the bottom piece. Finally, glue the candle on top of the cupcake, and finish it off by gluing the flame on top.

INSTRUCTIONS: CUPCAKE WITH CHERRY

1. TOP

Create a C-scroll using strip Ⓖ, as shown. Crease where indicated in the cutting guide. Rub the middle segment in the opposite direction of the curve (see photo at right) to create an indent.

2. ICING

Soften strip Ⓗ. Sharply crease where indicated, and then rub the middle segment to make it more curved. Coil both ends upward and then loosen them to create loose scrolls.

3. BOTTOM

Crease the folds and coil the ends of strip Ⓘ outward as shown to make the bottom part of the cupcake.

4. PLEATS

Zig-zag fold strip Ⓙ where indicated on the cutting guide, then scroll the ends outward. To achieve tight creases, use tweezers to compress the folds as shown in photo below at right.

Step 1

Step 2

Step 3

Step 4

Step 5

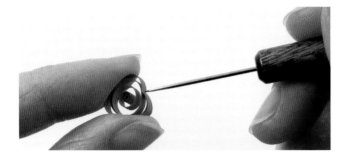

5. CHERRY

Create a very loose, 11 mm coil with strip (K).
Hold the circle between your thumb and index
finger, and use your quilling tool to push against
the glued end, just enough to make the dimple
on top of the cherry (see photo at left).

Glue the cherry into the indent in the top of
the cupcake.

6. STEM

Use strip (L) to create a loose scroll.

7. ASSEMBLY

Photocopy the cake stand template on the facing
page at 100% onto white card stock and trim at the
crop marks. Glue the bottom of the cupcake onto it
(using a ruler as a straight edge if needed). Glue the
top in place next, securing one end first and then
the other, so that both ends touch the top of the
bottom piece.

Place the icing strip inside the C-scroll that forms
the top, and adjust the size if necessary before gluing
it in place. Glue the pleats inside the bottom piece.
Finally, top it off by gluing the stem onto the cherry.

Step 6

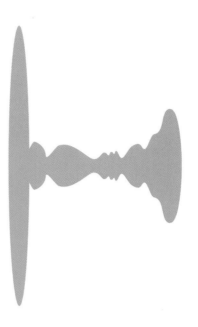

Bridal Shower

SKILLS YOU'LL NEED:
- Softening (page 7)
- Rubbing (page 7)
- Asymmetric S-scrolls (page 13)
- Scraping (page 7)
- Same-sided scrolls (page 12)

Project Components SKILL LEVEL: ● ● ● ● ●

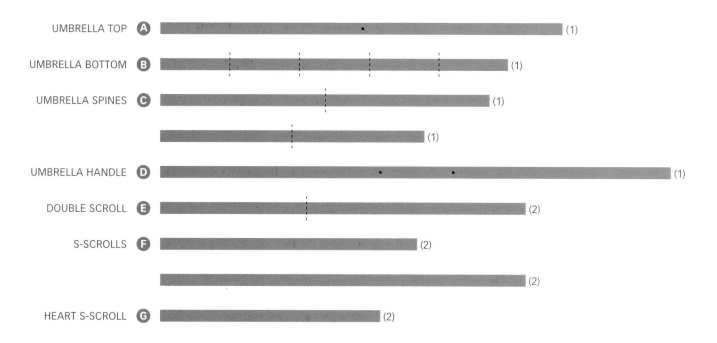

UMBRELLA TOP **A** ▬▬▬▬▬▬▬▬▬▬▬▬▬▬▬▬▬ (1)

UMBRELLA BOTTOM **B** ▬▬▬▬▬▬▬▬▬▬▬▬ (1)

UMBRELLA SPINES **C** ▬▬▬▬▬▬▬▬▬▬ (1)

▬▬▬▬▬▬▬▬ (1)

UMBRELLA HANDLE **D** ▬▬▬▬▬▬▬▬▬▬▬▬▬▬▬▬▬▬ (1)

DOUBLE SCROLL **E** ▬▬▬▬▬▬▬▬▬▬▬ (2)

S-SCROLLS **F** ▬▬▬▬▬▬▬▬▬ (2)

▬▬▬▬▬▬▬▬▬▬ (2)

HEART S-SCROLL **G** ▬▬▬▬▬▬▬ (2)

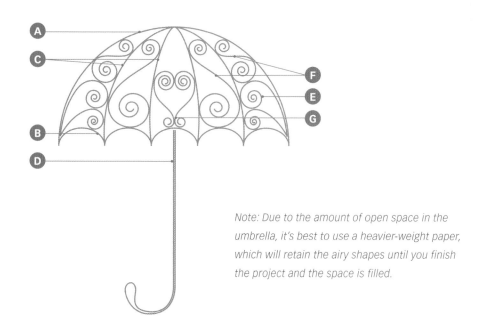

Note: Due to the amount of open space in the umbrella, it's best to use a heavier-weight paper, which will retain the airy shapes until you finish the project and the space is filled.

Step 2

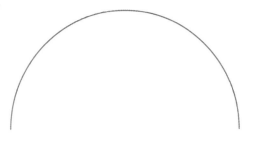

Step 3

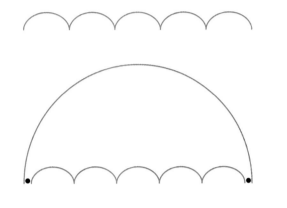

Step 4

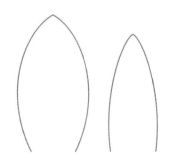

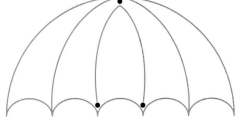

1. TEMPLATE

Photocopy the template on page 27 at 100% onto white cardstock, score along the dotted lines, and trim at the crop marks.

2. UMBRELLA TOP

Soften strip (A) into a curve as shown.

3. UMBRELLA BOTTOM

Scrape strip (B), and then sharply crease it along the dotted lines. Glue the ends of the umbrella bottom to the ends of the umbrella top.

4. UMBRELLA SPINES

Soften the (C) strips and sharply crease them where indicated.

Place the longer spine within the umbrella, gluing its point to the middle of the umbrella top, as indicated by the pencil mark you made on strip (A). Glue the ends into the outer creases in the umbrella's bottom.

Glue the point of the shorter strip to the center of the umbrella top as above, and then glue the ends of this spine into the center two creases of the umbrella bottom.

Now that you have the rest of your umbrella frame together, you can glue it to your card. Visually align the middle of the umbrella to the fourth heart from the left and glue it in place. (See the illustration at right.) Gluing the frame first will prevent it from moving as you add the inner elements.

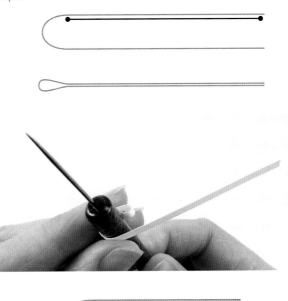

5. UMBRELLA HANDLE

Rub the space between the two pencil marks on strip Ⓓ so that it forms a U-shape strip. Thinly spread glue from the end to the pencil mark, as shown. Match up the ends of the strip and press them together.

While the glue is wet, curve the umbrella handle by wrapping it around your quilling tool (see photo at right).

Following the same angle as the rain, glue the handle in place.

6. DOUBLE SCROLL

Create two same-sided scrolls using the Ⓔ strips.

7. S-SCROLLS

Create four asymmetric S-scrolls using the Ⓕ strips.

Step 7

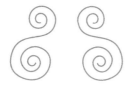

Step 8

Step 9

8. HEART S-SCROLL

Using the ⓖ strips, create two asymmetric S-scrolls with the smaller ends, quite tiny. Glue the heart together at the base as shown for ease of handling, but leave the top touching coils unglued so you can adjust them after you place them inside the umbrella.

9. ASSEMBLY

Before dipping the filler pieces in glue, nestle all of the scrolls into place, and then readjust them if necessary. Glue the scrolls in the same order as they were created. (See the illustration at left: Glue 1 first, 2 second, etc.) Finally, slip in a small dab of glue wherever the paper touches to strengthen the whole design.

SUGGESTED INSIDE MESSAGE:
Showering the bride-to-be with love!

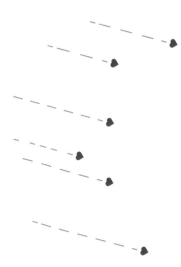

Wedding Cake

SKILLS YOU'LL NEED: • Heart scroll (page 12) • Softening (page 7)
• Loose coil (pages 8-9) • Asymmetric S-scroll (page 13)
• Scraping (page 7)

Project Components SKILL LEVEL: ●●●●●

TOPPER **A** ▭ (2)

ROSES **B** ▭ (6)

EMBELLISHMENT **C** ▭ (2)

RIBBON **D** ▭ ▭ ▭ (1)

BANNER (3PC) **E** ▭ (1) ▭ (1) ▭ (1)

BANNER (3PC) **F** ▭ (1) ▭ (1)

▭ (1)

TABLE (2PC) **G** ▭ (1)

▭ (1)

SPACER **H** ▭ (1)

TEMPLATE **I** ⬚

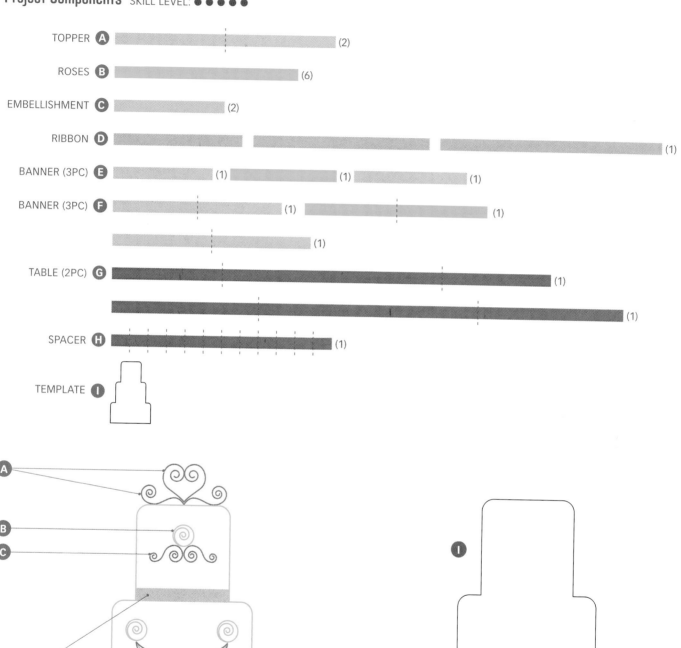

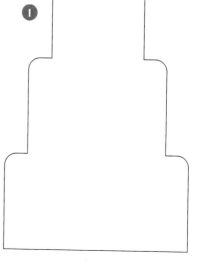

Step 2

Step 3

Step 4

Step 5

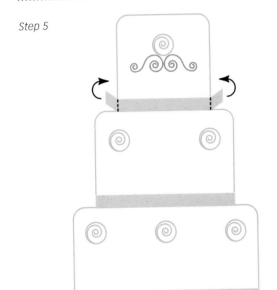

Step 6

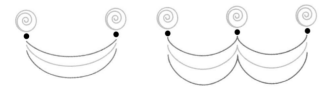

1. **TEMPLATE**

   Photocopy the cake template on page 29 and cut it out.

2. **TOPPER**

   Create two heart scrolls using the (A) strips. Glue one together so it looks like a heart, and soften the other heart scroll in the opposite direction on either side of the fold, as shown. Glue the heart into the center of the open heart scroll, as shown.

3. **ROSES**

   Use the (B) strips to create six loose 6 mm-coils.

4. **EMBELLISHMENT**

   Create asymmetric S-scrolls using the (C) strips. Glue the bigger ends together as shown, and then glue a rose on top of and between them.

5. **RIBBONS**

   Wrap the (D) strips around the base of each tier—the shortest one on the top tier, the longest on the bottom tier, etc. Since glue can seep through the ribbon, place your glue only on the ends on the back side of the cake. Glue the roses and embellishments onto the cake as shown at left.

6. **BANNERS**

   Scrape all three of the (E) strips. Glue the shortest of the three (E) strips to two roses (one end glued to each rose), and then repeat with the remaining two (E) strips. Using tweezers during this process will help with the placement.

   Do the same as above with three of the (F) strips.

7. TABLE AND SPACER

Coil up both ends of the two Ⓖ strips, and fold them down where indicated on the guide. Now, zig-zag fold strip Ⓗ along the lines indicated in the cutting guide. Sandwich the spacer between the two table pieces, gluing all three pieces together.

Finally, glue the edges of the table together, and glue the cake in place on the tabletop. Mount a 4½ x 6½-inch (11.4 x 16.5 cm) piece of pink card stock onto a white 10 x 7-inch (25.4 x 17.8 cm) card (folded in half to 5 x 7-inches [12.7 x 17.8 cm]), and then glue the cake to the center of the pink square.

Step 7

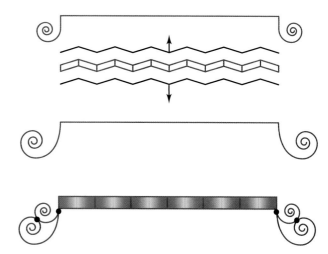

Baby Shower

SKILLS YOU'LL NEED:
- Softening (page 7)
- S-scroll (page 11)
- Heart scroll (page 12)
- Loose coil (pages 8-9)
- Crimping (page 7)
- Loose scroll (page 10)

Project Components SKILL LEVEL: ●●●○○

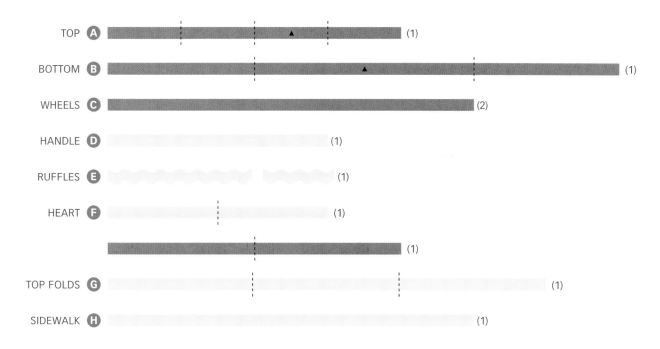

TOP **A** .... (1)

BOTTOM **B** .... (1)

WHEELS **C** .... (2)

HANDLE **D** .... (1)

RUFFLES **E** .... (1)

HEART **F** .... (1)

.... (1)

TOP FOLDS **G** .... (1)

SIDEWALK **H** .... (1)

Note: Instead of the blue I've used here, use the card background and colors from the bridal shower card (page 27) for a baby girl.

Step 2

Step 3

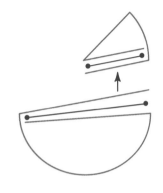

Step 4

Step 5

1. TEMPLATE

Photocopy the template on page 36 at 100% on cardstock and trim at the crop marks.

2. SIDEWALK

Scroll both ends of strip Ⓗ downward to create the sidewalk and glue it onto your photocopied template, about 2 inches from the bottom. While gluing in place, use a ruler to help guide and keep your strip straight and centered. The template on page 33 can be enlarged by 200% to use as reference for placement if you'd like.

3. BUGGY TOP AND BOTTOM

Crease the folds. Soften strips Ⓐ and Ⓑ to curve the segments marked with triangles (▲). Overlap the ends and glue them together as shown. Glue the top to the bottom.

4. WHEELS

Create two 10 mm loose coils with the Ⓒ strips and glue them to the buggy bottom as shown.

5. RUFFLES

Crimp and then cut the two Ⓔ strips and glue them to the buggy. The shorter one goes on the curved edge of the top piece, and the longer one goes along the straight edge of the bottom part.

6. TOP FOLDS

Soften the Ⓖ strip and sharply crease it where indicated. Dab a little glue in the folds and glue it together.

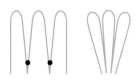

Put a little dab of glue on either side of the buggy top near the acute angle, as shown, one side at a time, gluing each end of the folds to secure the sides.

Dab a bit of glue into the buggy's acute corner and, using tweezers, push the two creases into the glue. Hold it in place until it's dry.

Glue the buggy on top of the sidewalk.

7. HANDLE

Create an S-scroll with strip Ⓓ and glue it in place next to the buggy as shown. Slide a dab of glue in between the touching areas to strengthen the design.

8. HEART

Create heart scrolls using the two Ⓕ strips. Nestle and glue the smaller one into the larger one, and then glue the top together as shown. Center the heart design in the buggy.

Step 7

Step 8

Ginkgo Condolence

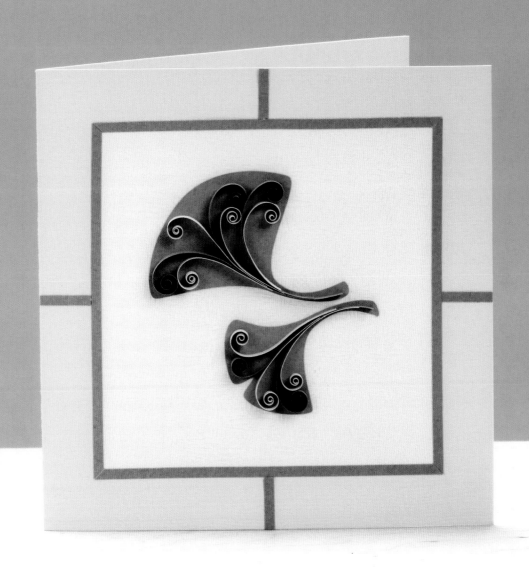

Project Components   SKILL LEVEL: ●○○○○

VEIN **A** ▬▬▬▬▬▬▬ (8)

VEIN **B** ▬▬▬▬▬▬▬▬ (3)

VEIN **C** ▬▬▬▬▬▬▬▬▬ (1)

LEAVES **D** (1)

FRAME **E** ▬▬▬▬▬ (4) ▬▬▬ (4)

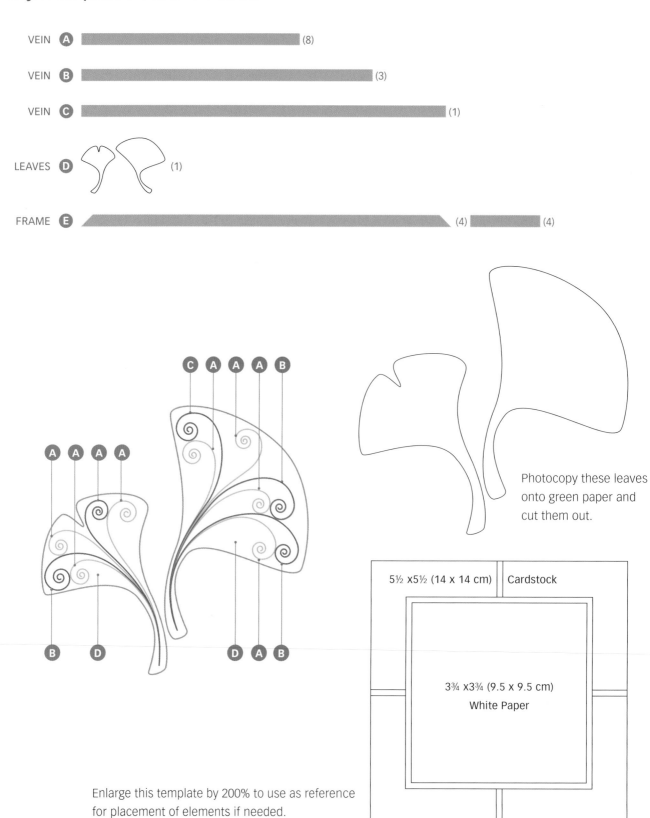

Photocopy these leaves onto green paper and cut them out.

5½ x5½ (14 x 14 cm)	Cardstock

3¾ x3¾ (9.5 x 9.5 cm)
White Paper

Enlarge this template by 200% to use as reference for placement of elements if needed.

1. TEMPLATE

Photocopy the ginkgo leaves on page 38 onto green paper and cut them out.

2. VEINS AND LEAVES

Soften all 12 strips you cut for veins (strips Ⓐ, Ⓑ, and Ⓒ) and create loose scrolls from all of them.

For the smaller leaf, glue vein Ⓑ first. For the larger leaf, glue vein Ⓒ first. As you add the remaining veins, they will follow the curve set by these first veins. Lengthen or shorten the strips as needed by tightening or loosening the scrolls. Pause to assess the placement and length before gluing permanently.

3. ASSEMBLY

To make the card background shown, start with a sheet of 11 x 5½-inch (27.9 x 14 cm) cardstock. Score and fold in half to make it 5½ x 5½ inches (14 x 14 cm). Cut a 3¾ x 3¾-inch (9.5 x 9.5 cm) sheet of white textured paper. Glue it to the middle of the card. Cut the Ⓔ strips and glue the longer ones around the white paper to make a frame as shown on page 38, bottom right. Glue the shorter Ⓔ strips last.

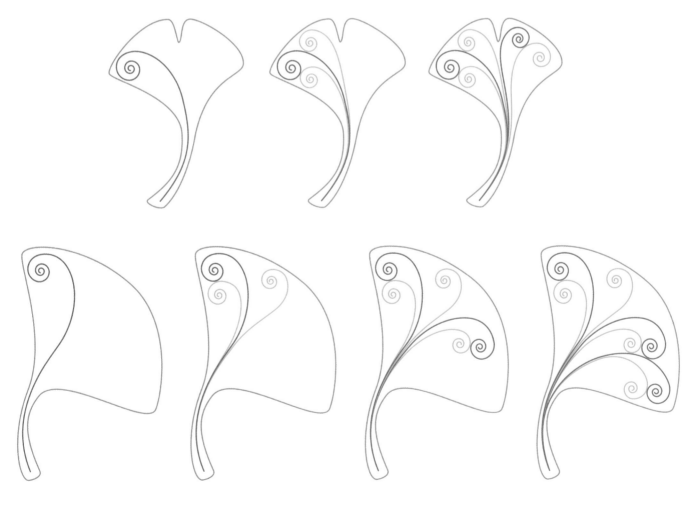

Happy Housewarming

SKILLS YOU'LL NEED:
- Loose scroll (page 10)
- Asymmetric C-scroll (page 13)
- S-scroll (page 11)
- Softening (page 7)
- Looser scroll (page 10)

Project Components SKILL LEVEL: ●●●●○

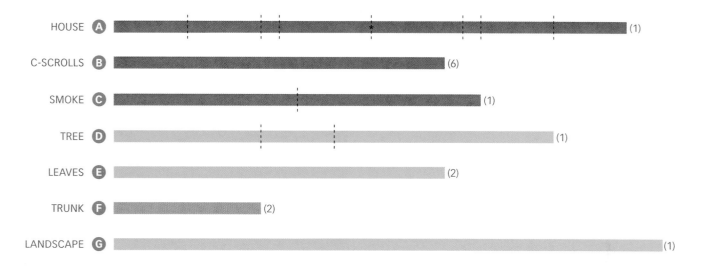

HOUSE **A** ————————————————— (1)

C-SCROLLS **B** ———————— (6)

SMOKE **C** ——————— (1)

TREE **D** ———————— (1)

LEAVES **E** ———————— (2)

TRUNK **F** ——— (2)

LANDSCAPE **G** ————————————————— (1)

Step 1

1. HOUSE

Crease the (A) strip as shown and scroll the ends upward. Place the house frame against a ruler to keep it even (see photo at left). Next, pin the sides of the house 1 inch (2.5 cm) apart, parallel to one another. Pin the eaves, and then pin the rooftop (indicated with an asterisk) last. Remove the pins as needed to put other elements in place.

2. C-SCROLLS

Create six asymmetric C-scrolls using the (B) strips, each with one end larger than the other. Place them within the house, adjusting the coils as needed to make them fit. Slide dabs of glue between the paper wherever it touches.

3. SMOKE

Fold the (C) strip as indicated and glue the ends together. Soften the doubled strip into a gentle curve, and then rub the middle section in the opposite direction (photo below, left). Separate the two strips, reshaping as needed (photo below, right).

Step 2

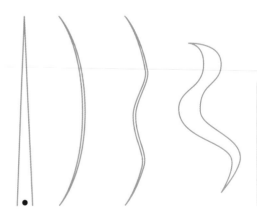

Step 3

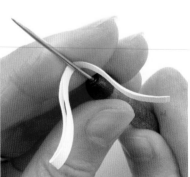

4. TREE AND TRUNK

Fold strip Ⓓ as indicated, soften it, quill the ends downward, and re-crease the folds. Create looser scrolls with the Ⓕ strips and glue them together as shown to make the tree trunk. Pin the trunk to prevent movement, and then glue the tree to the trunk.

5. LEAVES

Create two S-scrolls with the Ⓔ strips and place them within the tree. Slide glue between the paper wherever it touches.

6. LANDSCAPE

Soften the Ⓖ strip and coil it into an elongated S-scroll. (The landscape is shown here at 75%.)

7. ASSEMBLY

Loosely place your items on the final surface (a card or surface of your choosing). Make any adjustments necessary, and then glue the landscaping down. Next, glue the house so it sits on the higher part of the landscape. Place and glue the chimney smoke and tree last.

SUGGESTED INSIDE MESSAGE:
Congrats on your new home-sweet-home!

Step 4

Step 5

Step 6

Songbird Greeting

SKILLS YOU'LL NEED:
- S-scroll (page 11)
- Question-mark scroll (page 11)
- Softening (page 7)
- C-scroll (page 11)
- Same-sided scroll (page 12)

Project Components   SKILL LEVEL: ● ● ● ● ○

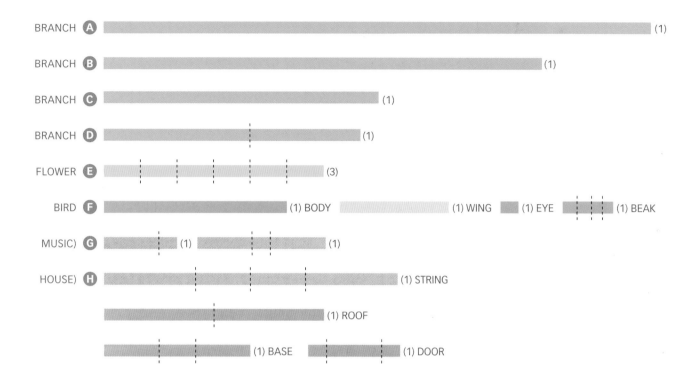

BRANCH **A** ▬▬▬▬▬▬▬▬▬▬▬▬▬▬ (1)

BRANCH **B** ▬▬▬▬▬▬▬▬▬▬▬ (1)

BRANCH **C** ▬▬▬▬▬▬▬▬ (1)

BRANCH **D** ▬▬▬▬▬▬▬ (1)

FLOWER **E** ▬▬▬▬ (3)

BIRD **F** ▬▬▬▬ (1) BODY   ▬▬▬▬ (1) WING   ▬ (1) EYE   ▬▬ (1) BEAK

MUSIC) **G** ▬▬ (1)   ▬▬▬ (1)

HOUSE) **H** ▬▬▬▬▬▬ (1) STRING

▬▬▬▬ (1) ROOF

▬▬ (1) BASE   ▬▬ (1) DOOR

Step 1

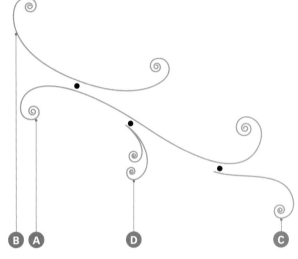

1. BRANCH

Create an S-scroll for (A), a C-scroll for (B), and a Question-Mark scroll for (C). Finally, make a Same-Sided scroll for (D).

Glue the pieces of the branch to your card one at a time in the order in which you made them. (The branch is shown at left at 75% actual size.)

2. FLOWERS

Sharply crease the folds of the (E) strips in a zigzag pattern. Soften the strip and re-crease the folds. Swing the last petal around to the first petal as shown. Place a dot of glue in the middle, securing all the folds. "Puff" out each petal by pushing the tip toward the center.

3. BIRD

Soften the (F) strip labeled as "Body" into a soft S shape. Bring one end up to meet the other and glue the ends together as shown. Repeat the same steps for the "Wing" strip. Glue the wing to the body. Next, rub the strip labeled "Eye" into a little arch. Finally, fold the "Beak" strip into an M shape as shown, and glue it and the eye to the bird.

Step 2

Step 3

4. MUSIC

Fold the (G) strips along the dotted lines on the cutting guide. Rub the top of the music symbols to give them a slight curve. Coil all the ends in the same direction.

5. HOUSE

To make the string from which the birdhouse hangs, fold the "String" (A) strip along the dotted lines on the cutting guide, and coil the ends up. Glue the two middle segments of the string together as shown, and set this piece aside.

For the roof, create a V-scroll with the "Roof" (H) strip and set it aside. Make the base of the house by folding the "Base" (H) strip along the dotted lines in the cutting guide and gluing the ends to the inside of the V-scroll you created for the roof. Now, glue the roof into the upside-down V-shape in the string piece.

The final piece is the door. Fold the "Door" (H) strip along the dotted lines and rub the middle segment to curve it. Glue the overlapping ends together as shown. Glue the door in the middle of the house.

SUGGESTED INSIDE MESSAGE:
Thinking of you makes me happy!

Step 4

Step 5

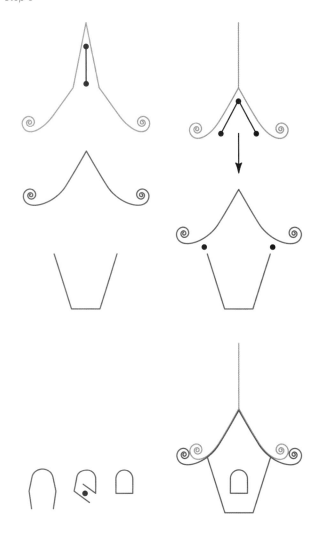

New Baby

SKILLS YOU'LL NEED: • Softening (page 7) • Same-sided scroll (page 12)
• Heart scroll (page 12) • Loose coil (pages 8-9)

Project Components SKILL LEVEL: ● ● ● ● ○

I've used pink for the cutting guide, but as you can see in the photo (left), you may simply switch it for blue or any other color.

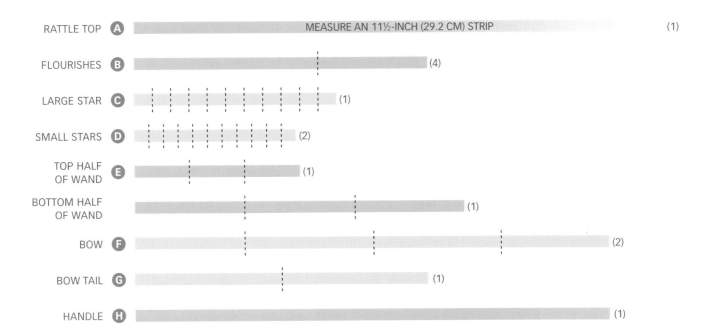

RATTLE TOP Ⓐ	MEASURE AN 11½-INCH (29.2 CM) STRIP	(1)
FLOURISHES Ⓑ		(4)
LARGE STAR Ⓒ		(1)
SMALL STARS Ⓓ		(2)
TOP HALF OF WAND Ⓔ		(1)
BOTTOM HALF OF WAND		(1)
BOW Ⓕ		(2)
BOW TAIL Ⓖ		(1)
HANDLE Ⓗ		(1)

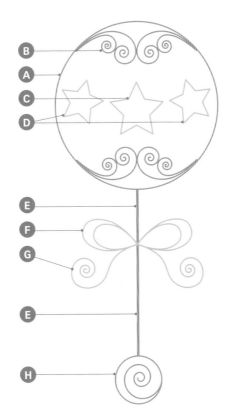

Step 1

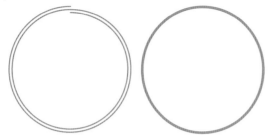

1. RATTLE TOP

Soften strip (A) and release it in a 1¾-inch (4.4 cm) circle template (75% of actual size shown). Glue the overlapping strip together to make a strong, double-thick circle. Keep the circle in the template to maintain its shape while you're adding the embellishments.

Step 2

2. FLOURISHES

Fold the four (B) strips as indicated, and then use them to create same-sided scrolls, tucking the shorter coil under the larger one. Pin the scrolls in place and then glue where the paper touches.

Step 3

3. STARS

Fold the (C) and (D) strips in a zig-zag pattern along the dotted lines in the cutting guide, creasing sharply. Overlap the ends as shown and glue each star closed.

Step 4

4. WAND

Crease the folds of the (E) strips in a zig-zag pattern and glue each one into a 3-ply piece for easier handling and increased gluing surface.

Step 5

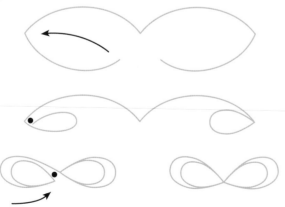

5. BOW

Soften the (F) strip and fold it as indicated in the guide. Tuck and glue the ends into the first folds like in the illustrations at left.

Now, flip the outermost folds toward the middle crease, gluing them in place.

6. BOW TAIL

Create a heart scroll with the (G) strip and then open up the fold as shown at right. Soften the middle area in the opposite direction (away from the inside of the heart). Glue the tail to the bottom of the bow.

7. HANDLE

Create a ½-inch (1.3 cm) loose coil with the (H) strip.

8. ASSEMBLY

Photocopy the polka-dot square below at 100%. Using the faint diagonal line as your guide, glue the rattle to the square. Place the circle template on the card and use it as a guide when gluing the rattle—it will keep your circle even. Working your way down, glue the remaining elements, starting with the top half of the wand, then the bow and the bottom half of the wand. Finally, glue down the handle and the stars.

Step 6

Step 7

Step 8

Color photocopy this background onto white card stock and cut along the outer frame.

Glue the finished piece to a matching 11 x 5½-inch (27.9 x 14 cm) piece of cardstock, folded in half to make a 5½ x5 ½-inch (14 x 14 cm) card.

Thank-You Bouquet

SKILLS YOU'LL NEED: • Loose coil (pages 8-9) • Softening (page 7)

Project Components   SKILL LEVEL: ● ● ● ○ ○

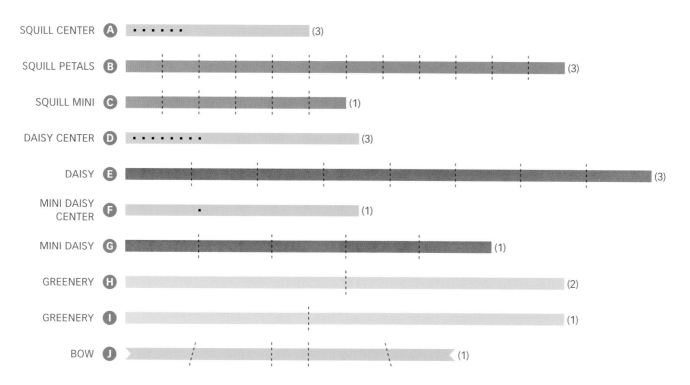

SQUILL CENTER Ⓐ `· · · · · · ·` (3)

SQUILL PETALS Ⓑ (3)

SQUILL MINI Ⓒ (1)

DAISY CENTER Ⓓ `· · · · · · · ·` (3)

DAISY Ⓔ (3)

MINI DAISY CENTER Ⓕ `·` (1)

MINI DAISY Ⓖ (1)

GREENERY Ⓗ (2)

GREENERY Ⓘ (1)

BOW Ⓙ (1)

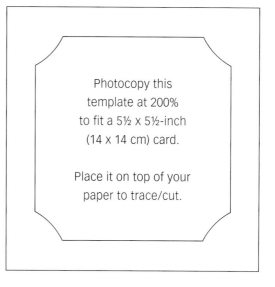

Photocopy this
template at 200%
to fit a 5½ x 5½-inch
(14 x 14 cm) card.

Place it on top of your
paper to trace/cut.

Step 1

Step 2 (Squills are shown here at 75%.)

Step 3

Step 4

Step 5 (Daisies are shown here at 75%.)

Step 6

1. SQUILL CENTERS

Starting from the end without pencil marks, create a loose scroll with one of the Ⓐ strips. Line up the end with the last pencil mark glue it closed. Repeat for the remaining two Ⓐ strips.

2. SQUILL PETALS

Sharply crease the folds of the Ⓑ strips in a zig-zig pattern. Soften and re-crease the folds. Glue the first fold to one of the pencil marks on the loose coil and allow it to dry. Next, match each fold up to a pencil mark on the coil, gluing one fold to the coil at a time.

3. SQUILL MINI

Sharply crease the folds of the Ⓒ strips in a zig-zig pattern. Soften the strip and re-crease the folds. Swing the last petal around to the first petal as shown. Place a dot of glue in the middle, securing all the folds. "Puff" out each petal by pushing the tip toward the center.

4. DAISY CENTERS

Create a loose scroll with one of the Ⓓ strips, line up the end with the innermost pencil mark so you can see the other seven pencil marks around the outside of the coil, and then glue it closed. Repeat for the remaining two Ⓓ strips.

5. DAISY

Soften each of the Ⓔ strips and crease the folds sharply. Glue them as you did the squill petals in step 2.

6. MINI DAISY CENTER

Create a loose scroll with the Ⓕ strip, line up the end with the pencil mark, and then glue the scroll closed to make a coil. Pinch both sides of the circle, creating two corners to form a half moon.

7. MINI DAISY

Soften the (G) strip and crease the folds sharply. Glue one end of it to the center, then the other end. Dab some glue in the middle as shown. Use tweezers to direct and hold the folds in place one at a time to form the small daisy.

8. GREENERY

Sharply crease the (H) strips where indicated, and then soften both halves of each strip together. Loosely coil the shorter half of each strip. Glue the fold together as shown at right (shown at 50%).

9. GREENERY

Repeat step 8 with the (I) strip but coil the longer segment this time instead of the shorter one.

10. BOW

Soften the (J) strip and sharply crease where indicated. Glue the outer folds to the bottom side of the inner folds. Scrape the two tails in the opposite direction and glue them to the bottoms of the bow loops.

11. ASSEMBLY

Glue the (I) greenery in between the two (H) greenery stems, and then glue two daisies and one squill on top of the stems as shown. Place the remaining flowers before gluing all the touching areas together. Glue the bow down on either side of the greenery stems. Finally, glue the entire bouquet to your card.

SUGGESTED INSIDE MESSAGE:

Thanks a bunch!

Step 7

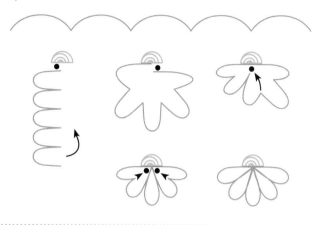

Step 8

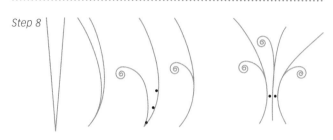

Step 10

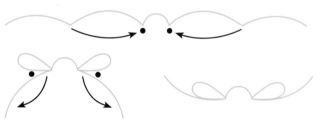

Step 11

Jam Jar Thank-You

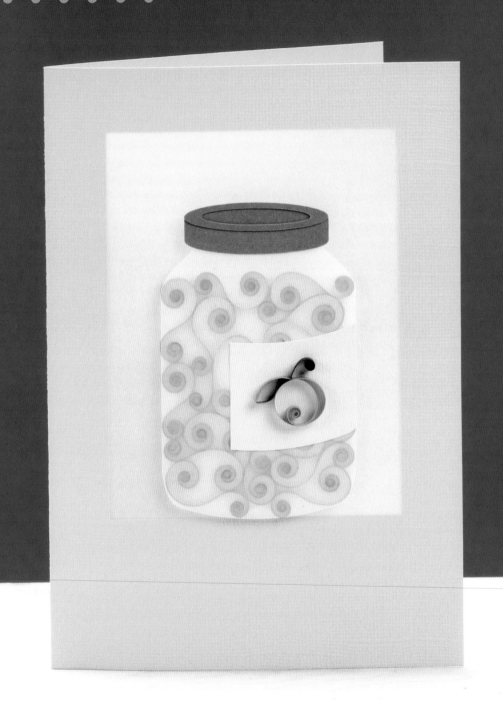

SKILLS YOU'LL NEED: • Loose scroll (page 10) • Softening (page 7)
• Asymmetric S-scroll (page 13)

Project Components   SKILL LEVEL: ●●●○○

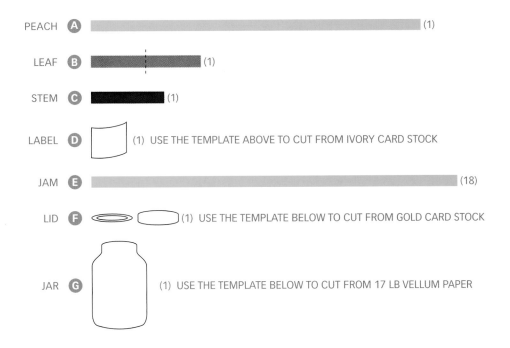

PEACH   **A** ▬▬▬▬▬▬▬▬▬▬▬ (1)

LEAF   **B** ▬▬▬▬▬ (1)

STEM   **C** ▬▬▬ (1)

LABEL   **D** ▭ (1) USE THE TEMPLATE ABOVE TO CUT FROM IVORY CARD STOCK

JAM   **E** ▬▬▬▬▬▬▬▬▬ (18)

LID   **F** ⬭ ▭ (1) USE THE TEMPLATE BELOW TO CUT FROM GOLD CARD STOCK

JAR   **G** (1) USE THE TEMPLATE BELOW TO CUT FROM 17 LB VELLUM PAPER

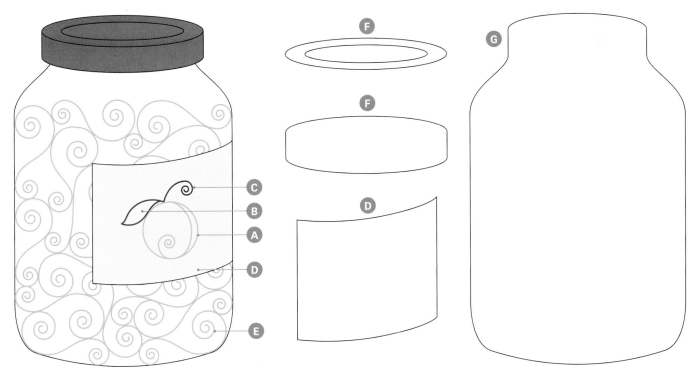

Step 2

Step 3

Step 4

Step 7

1. JAR COMPONENTS

Photocopy the lid template on page 57 onto gold card stock. Then copy the label template onto ivory card stock, and the jar onto 17-lb. vellum paper. They should all be copied at 100% (not enlarged or reduced).

2. PEACH

Create a 15 mm loose scroll with the Ⓐ strip, and glue the touching areas as shown.

3. LEAF

Crease the Ⓑ strip where indicated, and soften the doubled strip into a gentle S-shape. Separate the two halves and glue the ends together as shown. Glue your completed leaf to the peach.

4. STEM

Create a loose scroll using the Ⓒ strip and then glue it to the peach as shown.

5. LABEL

Cut out the label Ⓓ from your photocopied template and glue the peach onto it.

6. JAM

Create 18 asymmetric S-scrolls using the Ⓔ strips. The quantity of strips may need to be adjusted depending upon how tight or loose you make them.

7. LID

Cut out the two pieces for the lid Ⓕ from your photocopied template, and glue them together. The ring goes on top of the base. *(Lid shown here at 50%.)*

8. JAR

Cut out the jar shape (Ⓖ) from the vellum. Photocopy the template on the right to use as a placement guide on the jar. Note that it is backwards. This is because you'll be gluing the strips onto the backside of the vellum.

Place your jar-shaped piece of vellum on top of the guide template, and glue your S-scrolls in place as they are on the guide. You can be creative and glue the S-scrolls wherever you like, but the guide is there if you want it.

9. ASSEMBLY

After gluing each S-scroll in place, turn the jar over so the vellum is on top, and glue the label and the lid onto the jar.

I've also included an illustration of a 5 x 7-inch (12.7 x 17.8 cm) card, below right. Use the measurements from it to create the background for your jar, and then glue the jar onto it by dabbing glue here and there on the bottom side of your S-scrolls.

Step 9

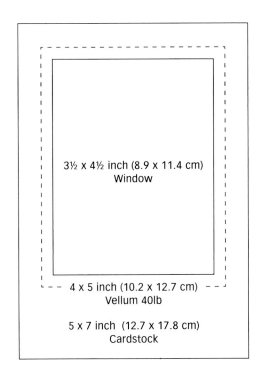

3½ x 4½ inch (8.9 x 11.4 cm)
Window

4 x 5 inch (10.2 x 12.7 cm)
Vellum 40lb

5 x 7 inch (12.7 x 17.8 cm)
Cardstock

Cherry Blossom Get-Well

SKILLS YOU'LL NEED: • Loose coil (pages 8-9) • Loose scroll (page 10)
• Softening (page 7)

Project Components SKILL LEVEL: ●●●○○

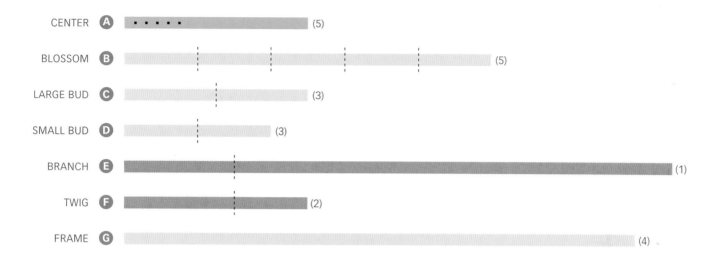

CENTER **A** ⋯⋯⋯ (5)

BLOSSOM **B** (5)

LARGE BUD **C** (3)

SMALL BUD **D** (3)

BRANCH **E** (1)

TWIG **F** (2)

FRAME **G** (4)

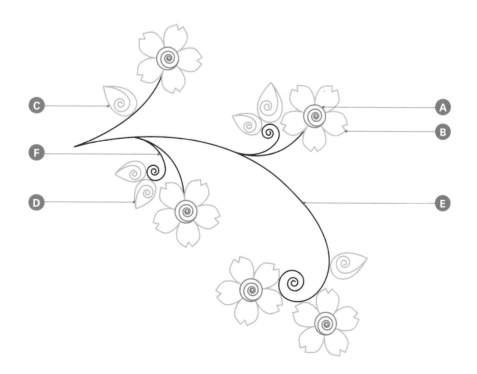

Step 1

Step 2

Step 3

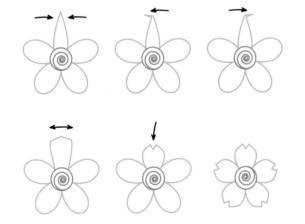

Step 4

1. CENTER

Starting from the end without pencil marks, create a loose scroll with one of the (A) strips. Line up the end with the last pencil mark and glue it closed. Repeat for the remaining four (A) strips.

2. BLOSSOM

Soften the (B) strip and re-crease the folds sharply. Dip the first fold into a puddle of glue. Press that fold against one of the pencil marks on the loose coil you made for the flower's center, using a toothpick to ensure good adhesion. While the glue is wet, gently press the flower on a flat surface to make the bottoms of the two pieces flush. Match each fold up to a pencil mark, gluing each one until only two ends remain loose. Finish by gluing one end at a time.

3. SHAPING THE PETALS

Pinch the rounded petal in the middle, resulting in a pointed petal. Using your tweezers, grip the petal tip and fold it left and then right, creating new creases. Open up the petal and push the tip inward to create a little "dent" in the end of each petal. Finally, gently push the two new tips toward the center of the flower to make the petals puff out and look fuller.

4. LARGE BUD AND SMALL BUD

Soften all six (C) and (D) strips and fold them in half as indicated in the guide. Create a loose scroll with one half of each strip, as shown at left. Wrap the other segment around the scroll and glue it closed. You will end up with three large buds and three small ones.

5. BRANCH

Soften the Ⓔ strip, fold it as indicated, and create a loose scroll at the end of the longer half, as shown. Glue the branch together.

6. TWIG

Soften both Ⓕ strips, fold them as indicated, and loosely scroll the longer segment of each one. Fold at the crease and glue the twig together.

7. FRAME

Glue the four Ⓖ strips parallel to, and ½ inch (1.3 cm) away from, the edges of a 5½-inch (14 cm) square card.

8. ASSEMBLY

Place all of the elements on your card first to gauge the space accurately. Glue the branch and twigs first, followed by the blossoms and buds.

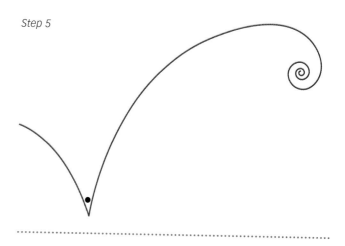

Step 5

Step 6

Dragonfly All-Occasion

SKILLS YOU'LL NEED: • Loose coil (pages 8-9) • Rubbing (page 7)
• Question mark scroll (page 11)

Project Components SKILL LEVEL: ●●●○○

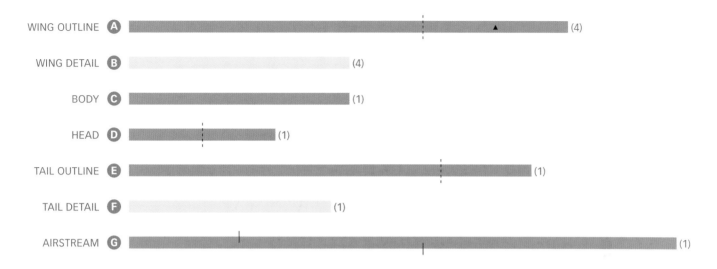

WING OUTLINE **A** ────────── (4)

WING DETAIL **B** ────────── (4)

BODY **C** ────────── (1)

HEAD **D** ────────── (1)

TAIL OUTLINE **E** ────────── (1)

TAIL DETAIL **F** ────────── (1)

AIRSTREAM **G** ────────── (1)

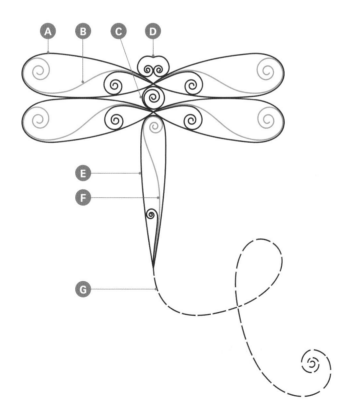

Step 1

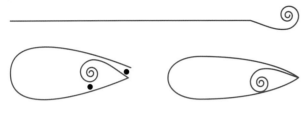

Step 2

Step 3

Step 4

1. WING OUTLINE

Soften one of the (A) strips, and create a loose scroll with the shorter segment (indicated in the cutting guide with a triangle [▲].

Fold the strip where indicated in the guide, and use the longer segment to form a loop that comes back around to the fold as shown, and glue it in place. Repeat these steps with the three remaining (A) strips. Hold the rounded end of each wing against your finger and use your tool to rub a defined curve (see photo at left) into it.

2. WING DETAIL

Create four question mark scrolls with the (B) strips and glue them into the wings as shown.

3. BODY

Create a 6 mm loose coil with the (C) strip to make the middle part of the dragonfly's body. Glue the wings to it, and then glue the wings to one another as shown.

4. HEAD

Create a V-scroll using the (D) strip. Turn the ends downward, then toward each other and glue the coiled ends together as shown. Glue the head onto the wings.

5. TAIL

Using strips (E) and (F), repeat steps 1 and 2 to assemble and embellish the tail, and then glue it onto the wings as shown. Dab the top edges of the completed dragonfly with a silver inkpad or paint pen.

6. AIRSTREAM

Soften the (G) strip, and then cut it as indicated in the guide. Make sure that the cuts are at least halfway into the strip as shown. Interlock the strip into itself (see photo at right). Coil the tail into whatever pattern you like, and dot the top edge of the flight path with a silver paint pen.

Step 5

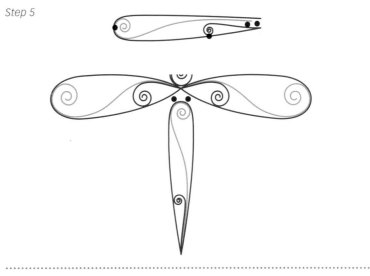

Step 6

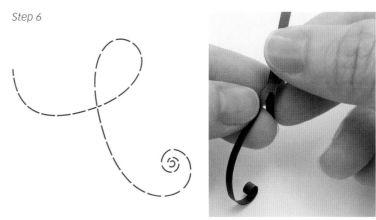

Topiary Trio All-Occasion

SKILLS YOU'LL NEED: • Heart scrolls (page 12) • Loose scrolls (page 10)
• Asymmetric S-scrolls (page 13) • Tight coils (page 10)

Project Components SKILL LEVEL: ●●●○○

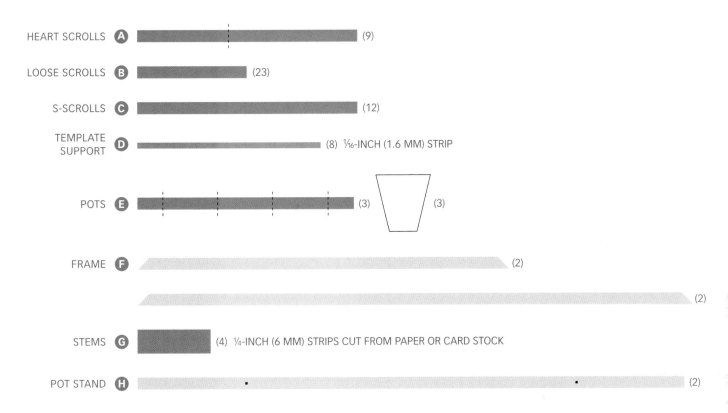

HEART SCROLLS **A** (9)

LOOSE SCROLLS **B** (23)

S-SCROLLS **C** (12)

TEMPLATE SUPPORT **D** (8) ¹⁄₁₆-INCH (1.6 MM) STRIP

POTS **E** (3) (3)

FRAME **F** (2)

(2)

STEMS **G** (4) ¼-INCH (6 MM) STRIPS CUT FROM PAPER OR CARD STOCK

POT STAND **H** (2)

Step 1

Step 2

Step 3

1. HEART SCROLLS, LOOSE SCROLLS, S-SCROLLS

Create nine heart scrolls from the (A) strips. Tuck the smaller segment under the longer, as shown, and leave them unglued so they can be moved around for any adjustments. Create 23 loose scrolls using the (B) strips. Create 12 asymmetric S-scrolls with the (C) strips.

2. TEMPLATE AND SUPPORT

Photocopy the template on page 71 at 100% onto cardstock and cut out the shapes. You're going to use the white space as a guide, so take care not to damage it as you cut and discard the shaded shapes. Next, create tight coils using the (D) strips (a total of eight) and glue them on the template's bottom as shown at left. The tight coils will act like little stilts to raise the template above the card's surface, creating a steady "fence" for the quilled shapes.

Center the template on your 5 x 7-inch (12.7 x 17.8 cm) card and secure it with removable tape. Starting from the top, fill each topiary with your quilled shapes. Fill the first tree on the left with the heart scrolls, the middle one with loose scrolls, and the one on the right with S-scrolls. Make the shapes larger or smaller as necessary so that they fit. When all are nestled in place, slide glue in between each touching area. When they're dry, use tweezers to pick up the topiary and glue it to your card permanently.

3. POTS

Trace and cut out three pot shapes from paper that's the same color as the (E) strips. Cardstock will work best for this, but any paper will do. Fold the strips as indicated in the guide and glue the overlap closed as shown at left. Glue the outlines so they frame the pot shapes. To help with alignment, place the pot outline and shape upside down on your work surface—this keeps one edge steady while you align the sides and bottom (see photo above left). Glue the pots to your card using the template as your guide.

4. FRAME

Cut the four Ⓕ strips at an angle, as shown in the cutting guide, and glue them along the outer edges of the template, removing and reattaching the tape as necessary. Once your frame is in place, you can remove the template.

5. STEMS

Wrap the four Ⓖ strips around a skewer, round toothpick, or a small crochet hook to create larger-circumference tight coils (see photo at right). Glue each coil closed before sliding it off of your tool, and then glue the tubes to your card where stems the should be with the seam side down.

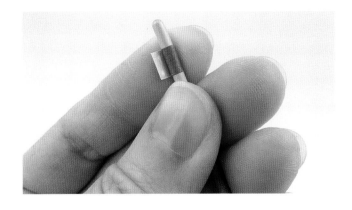

Step 6

6. POT STAND

Coil the ends of each Ⓗ strip in the same direction, stopping at the pencil marks you made. Match up the pencil marks on one with those on the other, and glue the two pieces together back to back so the pencil marks are hidden. Glue them to your card beneath the pots. (The stand is shown here at 75%.)

Photocopy this template at 100% onto cardstock and cut out the shapes. You'll be using the white space as a kind of "fence" to hold shapes together while you glue them.

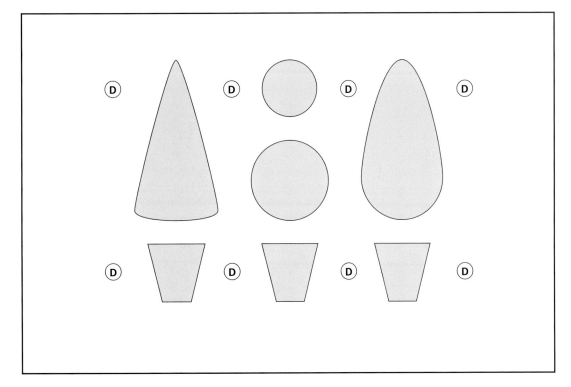

Valentine's Day Swing Card

SKILLS YOU'LL NEED: • Softening (page 7) • Heart scroll (page 12)
• V-scroll (page 12)

Project Components SKILL LEVEL: ●●○○○

LARGE HEART **A** ▬▬▬▬▬▬▬▬▬▬▬▬▬▬▬ (1)

LARGE HEART **B** ▬▬▬▬▬▬▬▬▬▬▬ (1)

LARGE HEART **C** ▬▬▬▬▬▬ (1)

SMALL HEART **D** ▬▬▬▬▬▬▬▬▬▬▬ (1)

SMALL HEART **E** ▬▬▬▬▬▬▬ (1)

SMALL HEART **F** ▬▬▬▬ (1)

V-SCROLL **G** ▬▬▬▬▬▬ (1)

V-SCROLL **H** ▬▬▬▬▬ (1)

Step 1

1. LARGE HEART

Use the Ⓐ, Ⓑ, and Ⓒ strips to make one large heart. Soften each strip, fold them in half, and then coil the ends to make tight heart scrolls. Stack the strips and glue them together at the middle fold. Uncoil and re-coil them by hand, allowing the curls to randomly wrap each other for a playful look. Glue all areas that touch one another in order to prevent the tornado effect (page 13) when you're gluing the final piece.

Step 2

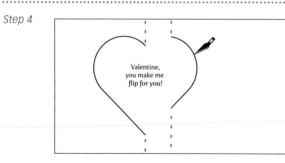

2. SMALL HEART

Use the Ⓓ, Ⓔ, and Ⓕ strips strips to make one small heart. Quill them just like you did Ⓐ, Ⓑ, and Ⓒ. Glue the large heart and the small heart together as shown at left.

Step 3

3. LARGE AND SMALL V-SCROLL

Soften the Ⓖ and Ⓗ strips, fold them in half, and then coil them to create your V-scrolls. Place one scroll above the other, gluing them together in the middle. Glue the places where the two V-scrolls touch one another.

4. ASSEMBLY

Photocopy the Valentine on the next page at 100% onto white cardstock. Score along each dotted line until it meets the heart outline. Trim at the crop marks and then cut along the solid lines as shown in the top illustration. Refer to the bottom illustration and fold along the dotted lines as indicated. Be careful to fold just the card, not the heart. Glue the hearts and flourishes onto the front side of the heart (previously the back side).

Step 4

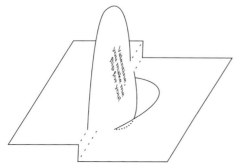

Valentine, you make me flip for you!

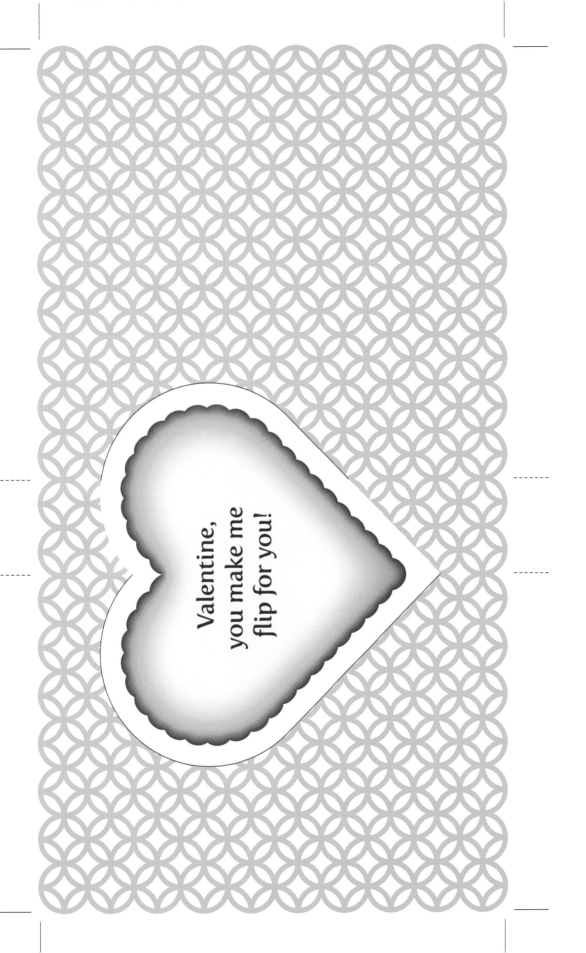

Valentine,
you make me
flip for you!

Mother's Day Vases

SKILLS YOU'LL NEED: • **Softening** (page 7)   • **Rubbing** (page 7)
                                    • **V-scroll** (page 12)   • **Loose coil** (pages 8-9)

Project Components   SKILL LEVEL: ●●●○○

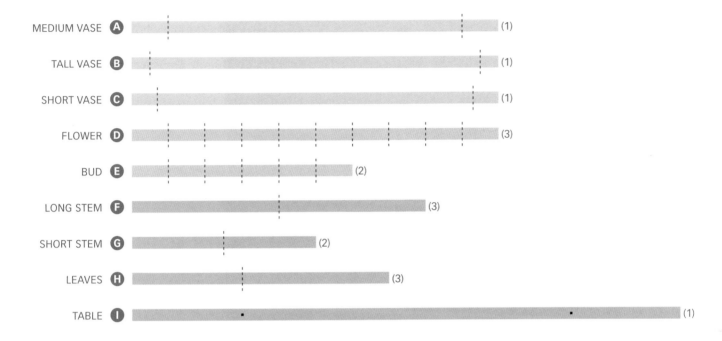

MEDIUM VASE Ⓐ	(1)
TALL VASE Ⓑ	(1)
SHORT VASE Ⓒ	(1)
FLOWER Ⓓ	(3)
BUD Ⓔ	(2)
LONG STEM Ⓕ	(3)
SHORT STEM Ⓖ	(2)
LEAVES Ⓗ	(3)
TABLE Ⓘ	(1)

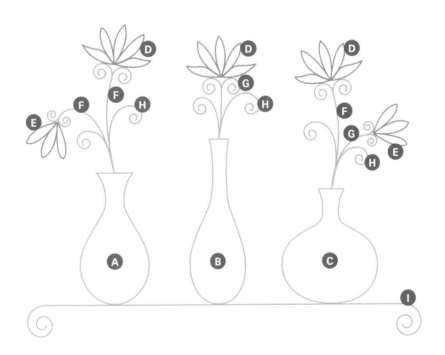

Step 1

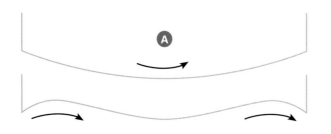

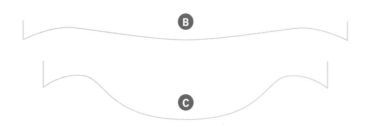

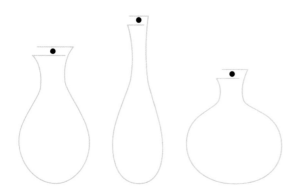

1. VASES

Soften the middle segment of the Ⓐ strip so that the ends curve upward (see diagram at left). Gently grasp the middle of the curve, and soften the ends of the middle section in the opposite direction so they curve back down, as shown. Repeat for strips Ⓑ and Ⓒ.

Bring the ends of each strip together and glue them (as shown below right) to form the vases. If adjustments are needed, use your quilling tool to scrape and rub the paper against your finger (top row of photos below). Finally, pinch the tops for a sharp crease (photo on bottom left).

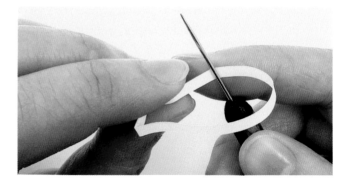

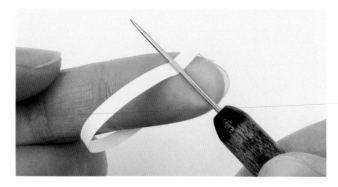

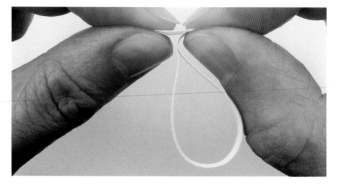

2. FLOWER AND BUD

Soften the Ⓓ and Ⓔ strips and crease them sharply along the folds as shown in the illustration at right.

Rotate one petal around to the other side so the ends meet as shown, thereby encapsulating all the petals. Dab some glue in the middle, securing all the folds and hold until dry.

"Puff" out each petal by pushing the tip toward the center. Turn the outermost petals upward by rubbing on the top side of their tips.

3. LONG STEM AND SHORT STEM

Create V-scrolls from each of the Ⓕ and Ⓖ strips, and then glue them in the middle to create your stems. Shape each one while the glue is still wet. Glue the flowers and buds to the stems.

4. LEAVES

Create V-scrolls from each of the Ⓗ strips. Making them asymmetrical gives them a more natural look. Glue the leaves to the stems at the base as shown.

5. TABLE

Coil both ends of the Ⓘ strip starting from the ends and coiling up to the pencil marks you made to create the table.

6. ASSEMBLY

Glue the table to your card first, using a ruler as a guide to help keep it even and straight. Space out the vases and glue them down. Arrange the flowers as desired, and glue them in place. (Finished piece is shown here at 50%.)

Gingerbread Couple

SKILLS YOU'LL NEED:
- Fringing (page 102)
- Scraping (page 7)
- Loose coil (pages 8-9)
- Tight coil (page 10)
- Crimping (page 7)

Project Components SKILL LEVEL: ●●●○○

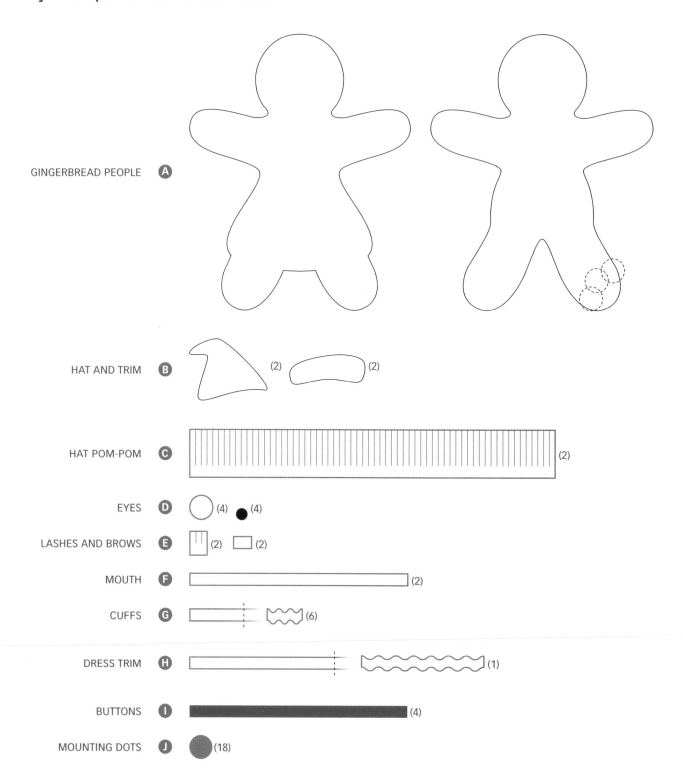

GINGERBREAD PEOPLE **A**

HAT AND TRIM **B** (2) (2)

HAT POM-POM **C** (2)

EYES **D** (4) (4)

LASHES AND BROWS **E** (2) (2)

MOUTH **F** (2)

CUFFS **G** (6)

DRESS TRIM **H** (1)

BUTTONS **I** (4)

MOUNTING DOTS **J** (18)

INSTRUCTIONS

1. GINGERBREAD PEOPLE

Photocopy the gingerbread couple (Ⓐ) onto cardboard (from a cereal box or the back of a note pad) and cut them out. Use a ¼-inch hole punch to make bite marks if desired. (The gingerbread people are shown above at 50%.)

2. HAT AND TRIM

Cut the hats (Ⓑ) from red paper and the hat trims from white paper. Glue the trims to the hats, and then glue the hats to the gingerbread couple.

Step 1

Step 2

Step 3

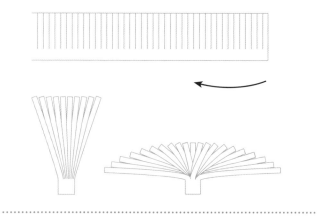

3. HAT POM-POM

Fringe (refer to step 10 on page 102 for fringing instructions) the two Ⓒ strips and, using a slotted quilling tool, curl each fringed strip into a tight coil. Fluff the pom-poms open, and then glue them to the hat tips.

4. EYES

Use a ¼-inch (6 mm) hole-punch to make four eyes from white paper, and use a ⅛-inch (3 mm) hole-punch to make four pupils from brown paper. Glue the pupils onto the eyes, and then glue the eyes to your gingerbread couple.

Step 4

5. LASHES AND BROWS

Fringe the two Ⓔ strips. Place the eyelashes on your finger and rub them back and forth to create a curl (see photo at left). Turn them sideways and rub them again to create a curl parallel to the eyes (see photo below left). Rub and press the brows just like you did the lashes.

Step 5

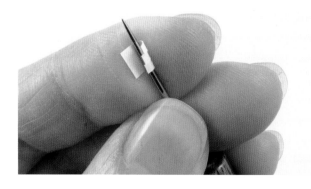

6. MOUTHS

Scrape one of the Ⓕ strips and release it in a 6.5 mm circle template. The strip will overlap itself about three times. Glue the overlapping areas to form a solid O-shape. Pinch on either side of the O-shape to form a smile. Or, if your ginger man has a chunk missing like mine does, maybe you want to keep the O-shape so he looks alarmed! (The mouth shown below is at 200%, so you can see the detail.) Repeat these steps with the other strip to make the second mouth.

Step 6

7. CUFFS AND DRESS TRIM

Fold strip Ⓖ onto itself four times, gluing the layers together. Crimp the strip while the glue is still wet. This will make your cuff look thick, as if it were icing.

Repeat these same steps with the Ⓗ strip to make the dress trim. Using your fingers, gently soften the trim into a curve to follow the dress outline.

8. BUTTONS

Using the Ⓘ strips, create four 7 mm loose coils for the buttons.

9. ASSEMBLY

Place all the pieces on the gingerbread couple and play around with their expressions before gluing them down. It's fun to be creative and make them a little different, but I've included a close-up of the face on one of mine so you can get an idea of how it all fits together. Prepare a 5 x 7-inch (12.7 x 17.8 cm) card (a 10 x 7-inch [25.4 x 17.8 cm] piece of cardstock folded in half), but don't glue anything down yet. I chose green for mine, but you may choose any color you like.

10. MOUNTING DOTS

Use a ¼-inch hole punch to punch out 18 holes (Ⓗ) from cardboard. Glue three dots together, and then glue each stack to the backs of the gingerbread couple's heads and legs. (The dot assembly is shown below at 200%.) Glue the completed gingerbread couple to your greeting card, and you're all done!

Step 7

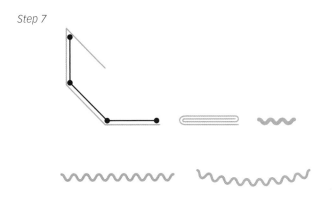

Step 8

Step 9

Step 10

Easter Basket

SKILLS YOU'LL NEED: • Softening (page 7)   • Crimping (page 7)

• Loose scrolls (page 10)

• Scraping (page 7)

Project Components SKILL LEVEL: ● ● ● ● ●

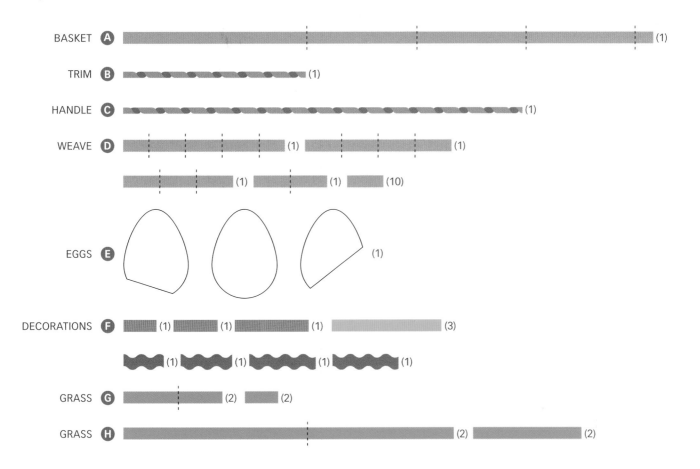

BASKET Ⓐ ── (1)

TRIM Ⓑ ●●●●●●●●●●●●●●● (1)

HANDLE Ⓒ ●●●●●●●●●●●●●●●●●●●●●●●●●●●●● (1)

WEAVE Ⓓ ▬▬▬▬▬ (1) ▬▬▬▬ (1)

▬▬▬ (1) ▬▬ (1) ▬ (10)

EGGS Ⓔ (1)

DECORATIONS Ⓕ ▬ (1) ▬ (1) ▬ (1) ▬▬▬ (3)

〰 (1) 〰 (1) 〰 (1) 〰 (1)

GRASS Ⓖ ▬▬ (2) ▬ (2)

GRASS Ⓗ ▬▬▬▬▬ (2) ▬▬▬ (2)

Step 1

Step 2

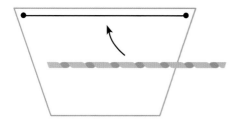

1. BASKET

Fold and glue strip Ⓐ as shown at left.

2. TRIM

Soften a full, uncut strip of quilling paper at an angle (see top left photo).

Thread the needle tool handle in between the three smaller fingers of your dominant hand (see middle photo at left).

The same hand will use the thumb and index finger to guide the strip and provide tension (see bottom photo at left). Your opposing thumb and index finger will twist the strip around the needle tool and gently push upwards and off the needle. Continue twisting the entire length of paper. Practice and even tension will yield a consistent spiral. It may take some time to master this technique, but it's worth the effort.

Lay your spiral against the template on page 87 and cut it, selecting the best parts of your spiraled strip as the lengths you'll use. Cut the shorter length for the basket's trim first, and then run a line of glue under the basket's rim to adhere the trim. (See illustration, below left.)

Glue the basket to a 4½-inch-(11.4 cm) square piece of ivory paper to help the elements stay in place. Glue the ivory sheet to a 4¾-inch-(12 cm) square piece of yellow paper, and then glue the yellow paper to a 6-inch-(15.2 cm) square piece of purple cardstock.

3. HANDLE

Create a spiraled strip for the handle using the spiraling technique from step 2. Cut the needed spiral length for the handle, and glue its ends to the card, against the basket. Using tweezers, lift the handle up and dab glue along the bottom spirals. Carefully settle the handle down in place.

4. WEAVE

Soften the (D) strips and sharply crease the folds to achieve curved arches. Space the (D) strips horizontaly and evenly within the basket. Using a fine-tipped glue applicator, glue the bottom of the arches to the card.

Using tweezers, dip the ends of the remaining 10 vertical strips into a small puddle of glue. Carefully glue them in place in between the arches, hiding the ends under the neighboring arches where applicable.

5. EGGS

Trace the three eggs onto colored paper and cut them out. Glue them together as shown, using a ruler to keep the two bottom eggs aligned.

6. DECORATIONS

Soften the three pink (F) strips and glue the curves to the orange egg.

Using the three yellow (F) strips, create loose scrolls and glue them to the pink egg.

Crimp the four purple (F) strips and, using the guide on page 87, cut the required lengths. Using your fingers, gently curve them to fit the egg and place them in the yellow egg as shown. Check the position before gluing them down.

Glue the decorated eggs to the card.

Step 3

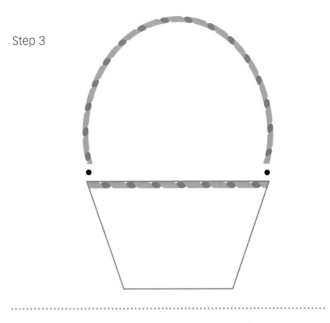

Step 4

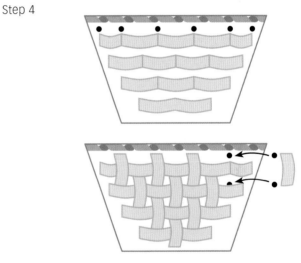

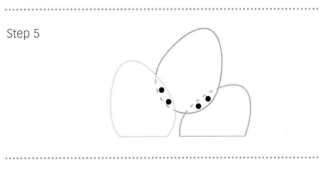

Step 5

Step 6

Step 7

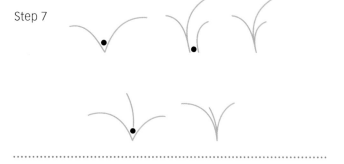

7. SMALL GRASS

Soften the Ⓖ strips and sharply crease the folds. For the first clump of grass, dab a small amount of glue inside the fold and glue it together. Glue the smaller strip to the outside of this V-fold as shown at left.

For the second clump of grass, dab a small amount of glue inside the fold. Insert the smaller strip and glue all of the pieces together as shown at left. Glue both clumps of grass in between the eggs.

8. LARGE GRASS

Glue the Ⓗ strips together as shown at left. Grasping the joined ends in one hand, scrape all three layers at one time. Separate the blades of grass to your liking and glue them to the card.

Step 8

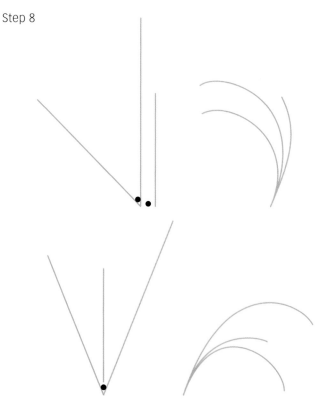

Father's Day Ties

SKILLS YOU'LL NEED:
- S-scrolls (page 11)
- Softening (page 7)
- Tight coils (page 10)
- Rubbing (page 7)

Project Components SKILL LEVEL: ●○○○○

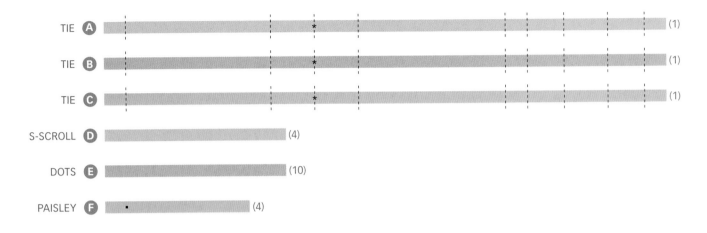

TIE **A** (1)

TIE **B** (1)

TIE **C** (1)

S-SCROLL **D** (4)

DOTS **E** (10)

PAISLEY **F** (4)

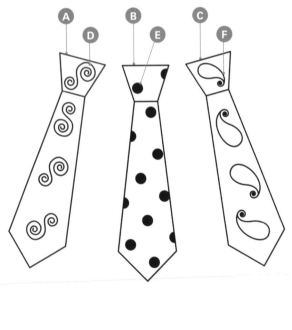

Color photocopy the paint strokes at 100% onto your paper. Cut along the outline and glue the paper onto a 5½ x 5½-inch (14 x 14 cm) card.

Step 1

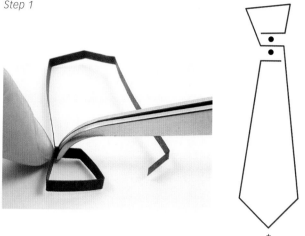

1. TIE

Fold and glue strips (A), (B), and (C) as shown. Use tweezers to align the edges against your fingernail (see photo at left). Glue the ties on top of the paint strokes of the template on the previous page. The (*) indicates the tip of the tie.

Step 2

2. S-SCROLL

Create four S-scrolls using the (D) strips, and then glue them within the green tie as shown. (I made my S-scrolls asymmetric, but you can make regular S-scrolls. See page 13 for more on asymmetric S-scrolls.)

Step 3

3. DOTS

Create 10 tight coils using the (E) strips. To make the polka-dotted tie look realistic, make some half dots to go on the edges of it. Start by covering two coils with glue as shown in the photo at left and allowing them to dry. Once they're dry, use a craft knife to vertically cut them in half. Glue the coils onto the blue tie, placing the four half dots at the edges as shown in the diagram on the previous page.

4. PAISLEY

Soften the (F) strips into four "S" shapes. On each of those four strips, glue the long end to the pencil mark you made, and coil the end. Gently rub the paisleys against your finger to define the curve (see photo at left) to your liking. Glue the paisleys onto the purple tie, one on the top and three on the long part of the tie.

Step 4

North Star

SKILLS YOU'LL NEED: • Loose scroll (page 10) • Softening (page 7)
• Rubbing (page 7)

Project Components SKILL LEVEL: ● ● ● ○ ○

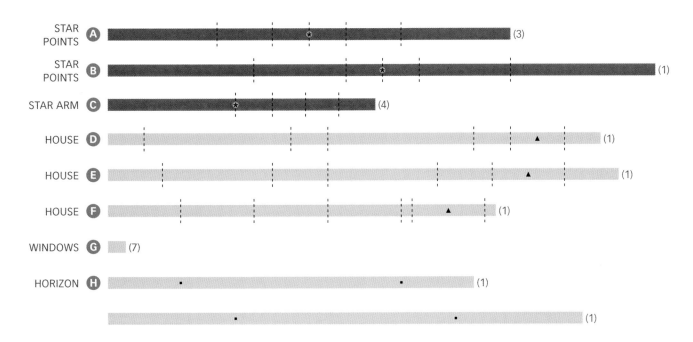

STAR POINTS **A** (3)

STAR POINTS **B** (1)

STAR ARM **C** (4)

HOUSE **D** (1)

HOUSE **E** (1)

HOUSE **F** (1)

WINDOWS **G** (7)

HORIZON **H** (1)

(1)

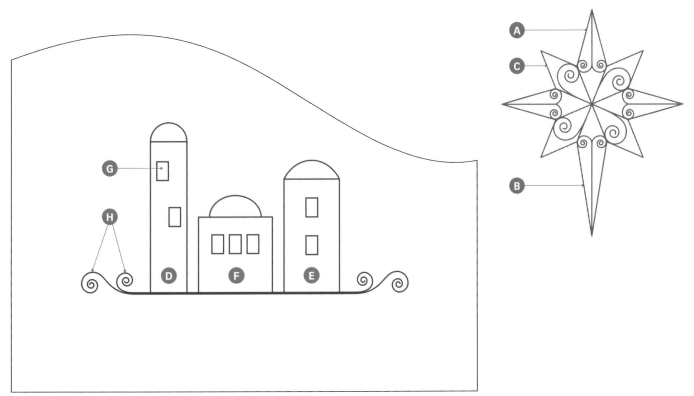

Step 1

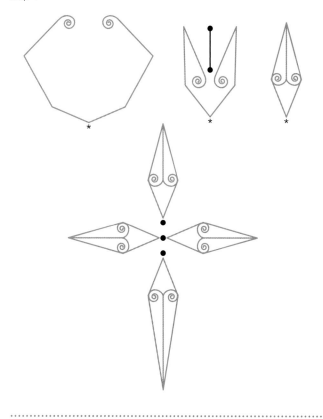

1. STAR ARMS

Scroll the ends of all four Ⓐ and Ⓑ strips, up to about half the length of the end segments. The asterisk (*) designates the star's center. Fold and glue each strip as shown at left.

Glue two of the small diamond shapes Ⓐ together first to form the sides, and then add the top and bottom pieces. The bigger diamond shape Ⓑ goes on the bottom. Pinning the pieces in place can really help you keep things consistent. (See page 6 for more info on pinning.)

2. SMALL STAR ARMS

Scroll the longest segment of each Ⓒ strip to the first fold. Fold and glue them as shown.

Place each of the four small diamond shapes into the empty spaces in the star, as shown. Glue all areas that touch. Waiting until this stage to glue the scrolls allows for adjustments so you can be sure everything is symmetrical.

Step 2

3. HOUSES

Starting with strip Ⓓ, rub to curve the segment indicated by the triangle (▲) on the paper-cutting guide, and then fold as shown. Glue the top of the house closed, and then glue the roof down as shown. Repeat with strip Ⓔ.

4. HOUSE

Rub the segment on strip Ⓕ indicated by the triangle (▲) on the paper-cutting guide so that it curves. Fold as shown and apply a couple of dabs of glue, adhering the roof and completing the house.

5. WINDOWS

Cut seven matching rectangles of paper from the Ⓖ strip, as shown.

6. HORIZON

Coil the ends of the Ⓗ strips as far as the pencil marks you made. Face the marks inward so they will be hidden after gluing, as shown. They should be on the bottom of the top strip and on the top of the bottom strip.

7. ASSEMBLY

Trace and cut the rolling hills background (page 95) out of your chosen paper. Using a ruler as a guide, glue the horizon line first, and then glue the houses on top. Use tweezers to glue the windows in place. Glue this scene to the bottom half of a 10 x 7-inch (25.4 x 17.8 cm) piece of cardstock, folded in half to make a 5 x 7-inch (12.7 x 17.8 cm) card. Glue the star near the top to complete your card.

Step 3

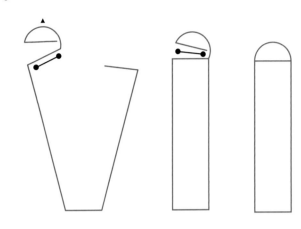

Step 4

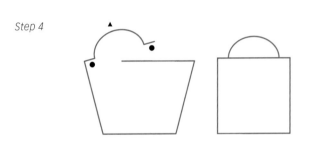

Step 6

Snowman

SKILLS YOU'LL NEED: • Softening (page 7) • Loose scroll (page 10) • C-scroll (page 1
• Tight coil (page 10) • Rubbing (page 7) • Scraping (page
• S-scroll (page 11)

Project Components SKILL LEVEL: ● ● ● ● ○

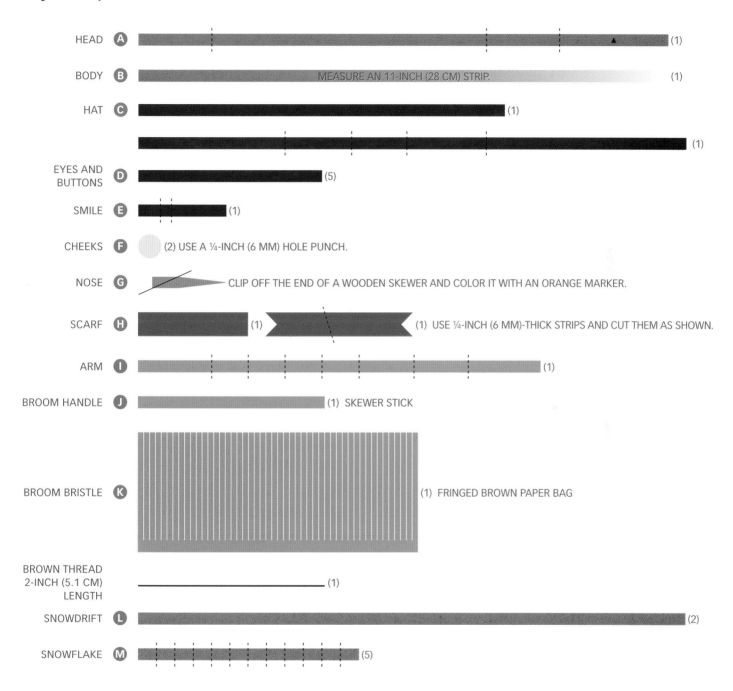

HEAD **A** (1)

BODY **B** MEASURE AN 11-INCH (28 CM) STRIP. (1)

HAT **C** (1)

(1)

EYES AND BUTTONS **D** (5)

SMILE **E** (1)

CHEEKS **F** (2) USE A ¼-INCH (6 MM) HOLE PUNCH.

NOSE **G** CLIP OFF THE END OF A WOODEN SKEWER AND COLOR IT WITH AN ORANGE MARKER.

SCARF **H** (1) (1) USE ¼-INCH (6 MM)-THICK STRIPS AND CUT THEM AS SHOWN.

ARM **I** (1)

BROOM HANDLE **J** (1) SKEWER STICK

BROOM BRISTLE **K** (1) FRINGED BROWN PAPER BAG

BROWN THREAD 2-INCH (5.1 CM) LENGTH (1)

SNOWDRIFT **L** (2)

SNOWFLAKE **M** (5)

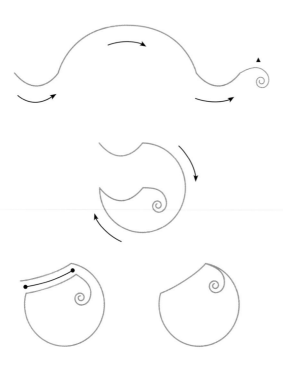

Step 1

INSTRUCTIONS

1. HEAD

Soften the (A) strip one segment at a time, in opposite directions, as shown. Scroll the segment indicated by the triangle (▲), and then loosen the coil.

Swing the third segment around under the first segment, curling the coiled end in toward the center, as shown, and then glue the overlapping areas together.

2. BODY

Soften the Ⓑ strip and release it within a 1¾-inch (4.4 cm) diameter circle template. It should overlap itself once, creating a circle that is two strips thick instead of one. Glue the overlapping paper together to create a stronger circle and maintain its shape. Glue the head and body together.

3. HAT

Create a C-scroll using the shorter of the two Ⓒ strips.

Soften the second Ⓒ strip and crease the folds sharply. Create inward-facing loose scrolls with the ends. Glue the two scrolls together and then to the right-hand side of the hat, as shown. Glue the C-scroll you made with the first strip to the bottom of this shape to finish the hat.

4. EYES, BUTTONS

Create tight coils from all five of the Ⓓ strips, and pinch two of them into ovals to make the eyes.

5. SMILE

Soften the Ⓔ strip, fold it where indicated, and then glue it together as shown.

6. CHEEKS

Use a ¼-inch (6 mm) hole punch to create cheeks (Ⓕ).

7. NOSE

Using a craft knife or sharp scissors, trim the sharp end of a skewer off at the angle shown in the paper-cutting guide. Use a nail file to smooth the cut so it will stick better when you glue it. Use an orange marker to color it.

8. SCARF

Soften the first Ⓗ strip, and then rub the ends of it downward so it appears to wrap around the snowman's neck. Dip the edges into glue and adhere it on either side of the neck.

Fold the second Ⓗ strip as shown and glue it together. Trim the fold, and scrape the notched ends to mimic wind blowing through the scarf.

Step 2

Step 3

Step 4

Step 5

Step 6

Step 8

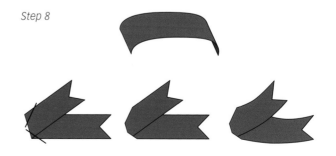

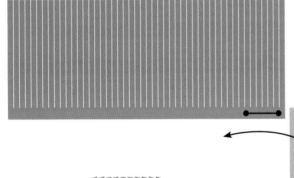

9. ARM

Fold and glue the (I) strip as shown. Rub the "fingers" to soften them. The arm should lie flat against the snowman (not on its edge).

10. BROOM HANDLE AND BRISTLES

Trace the rectangle ((K)) from the guide on page 99 onto a brown paper bag and cut it out. Lightly draw a pencil line ⅛ inch (3 mm) away from the edge, as shown. Using scissors, cut straight narrow lines up to the pencil line (see photo at left).

Glue the skewer stick onto the rectangle where you would place your quilling tool if you were going to make a tight coil with just that ⅛-inch-(3 mm) wide bottom strip, as if the bristles weren't even there. Create a tight coil with that bottom strip. Tie the bristles near the bottom with the length of brown thread. Fan the bristles out and tape the radiating paper in place—the tape side should face down when you glue the broom to your card.

11. SNOWDRIFT

Create S-scrolls using the Ⓛ strips. Stack them in an offset way, as shown, and glue them together where the paper touches.

12. SNOWFLAKE

Zig-zag fold the five Ⓜ strips as shown. Pull the ends of one of the strips together so it looks like a six-pointed star, and then glue each point closed to complete one snowflake. Repeat these steps with the remaining strips.

13. ASSEMBLY

The best way to assemble Mr. Snowman is to place all of the elements on your card without gluing them, to get a sense of spacing. Then remove one element at a time, dip it into glue, and adhere it permanently. The order isn't crucial, but you can use the order in which you assembled each piece.

Step 11

Step 12

Two Hearts Place Card

SKILLS YOU'LL NEED: • Asymmetric heart scrolls (page 13)

Project Components SKILL LEVEL: ●○○○○

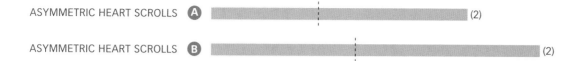

ASYMMETRIC HEART SCROLLS **A** �⸺⸺⸺⸺⸺⸺⸺⸺▪ (2)

ASYMMETRIC HEART SCROLLS **B** ▪⸺⸺⸺⸺⸺⸺⸺⸺ (2)

Photocopy this template at 100% onto the cardstock of your choice. Use scissors to cut the outer frame, and a craft knife to cut the hearts along the solid lines. Use a dried-up pen or an awl to score along the dotted lines.

Step 1

1. ASYMMETRIC HEART SCROLLS

Fold the (A) and (B) strips as indicated, and then make them into asymmetric heart scrolls, tucking the smaller coils into the larger ones.

Set the small scrolls on your work surface facing each other, they should mirror one another, and then glue them together. Do the same with the larger scrolls. Dab glue where the paper touches to secure the pieces in place, and then glue them to your place card as shown below, one heart at a time.

Wine Glass Charms

Project Components SKILL LEVEL: ●●○○○

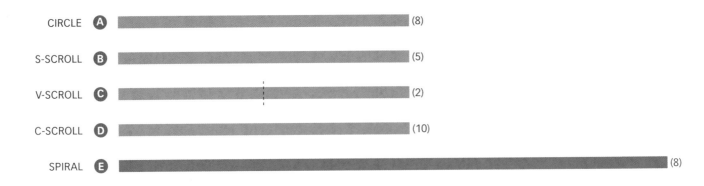

CIRCLE **A** ▬▬▬▬▬▬▬ (8)

S-SCROLL **B** ▬▬▬▬▬▬ (5)

V-SCROLL **C** ▬▬▬┆▬▬▬ (2)

C-SCROLL **D** ▬▬▬▬▬▬ (10)

SPIRAL **E** ▬▬▬▬▬▬▬▬▬ (8)

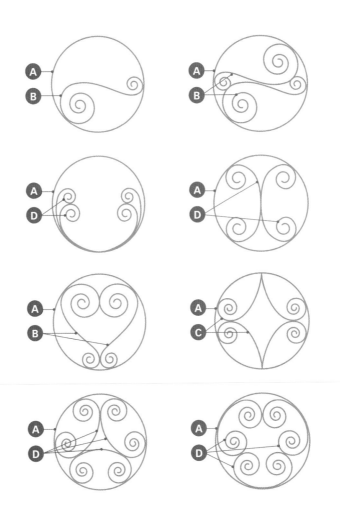

1. CHARM OUTLINE

You're going to make a total of eight charms, hence the eight Ⓐ strips for outlines. Soften the eight strips and release each of them in a 1-inch (2.5 cm) circle template. Glue the overlapping ends closed.

2. S-SCROLL

Create asymmetric S-scrolls with the Ⓑ strips and place them within three of the outlines as shown. To strengthen the design, dab glue between all areas where the paper touches. Make sure to keep the glue away from the top of the strips so that no glue shows.

3. V-SCROLL

Fold the two Ⓒ strips as indicated in the guide, and use them to create V-scrolls. Place them within the outlines, as shown. Glue any touching areas.

4. C-SCROLL

Using the Ⓓ strips, make 10 C-scrolls, six of them more tightly re-coiled than the other four (see the illustrations at right). Place them within four of the outlines as shown. Glue all touching areas.

5. CHARM ASSEMBLY

Cut eight 1⅜-inch (3.5 cm) circles from black cardstock, or whatever color you'd like. Place your plastic 1-inch circle template on top of the black circle to use as a guide when gluing your charm. This will help you keep it circular and centered. Glue the completed charms in the middle.

6. SPIRAL

Wrap the spiral around a chopstick or a pen, scrolling it at an angle so it looks like a spring. Slide it off and glue one end of it onto the back of the tag. Gently wrap the spiral around your wine glass stem.

Step 1

Step 2

Step 3

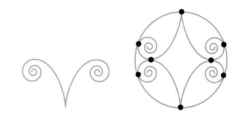

Step 4

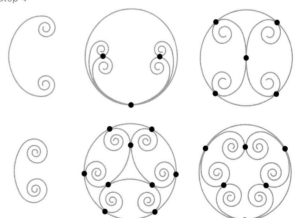

Step 5

Cupcake Toppers

SKILLS YOU'LL NEED:
- Loose coil (pages 8-9)
- Softening (page 7)

Project Components SKILL LEVEL: ●●○○○

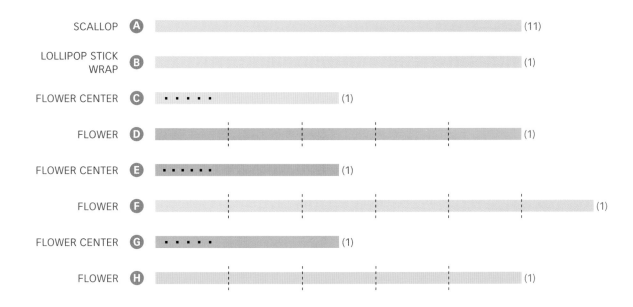

SCALLOP **A** (11)

LOLLIPOP STICK WRAP **B** (1)

FLOWER CENTER **C** · · · · · (1)

FLOWER **D** (1)

FLOWER CENTER **E** · · · · · · (1)

FLOWER **F** (1)

FLOWER CENTER **G** · · · · · (1)

FLOWER **H** (1)

To keep things simple, the instructions are for one cupcake topper. Triple all the quantities to make all three, and as always, feel free to improvise with your colors.

Step 2

Step 3

Step 5

Step 6

1. TEMPLATES

Color copy the blank circle and greeting circle (one of each) of your choice from the following page, and cut them out around the outside edges. Alternatively, you could choose two blank ones.

2. SCALLOP

Use the 11 (A) strips to make 10 mm loose coils. Glue the coils on the back in a circle so that half of each coil is on the tag and half hangs off, as shown. Leave a gap at the bottom for the lollipop stick.

3. LOLLIPOP STICK WRAP

Wrap the (B) strip around the lollipop stick as shown, and glue the ends in place. Glue about ¼ inch of the stick to the scalloped circle.

4. FLOWER TOP

Glue your greeting circle or second blank circle onto the back of the scalloped circle so that the coils are sandwiched between the two circles and the decorative side of each circle faces out.

5. FLOWER CENTER

Choose a flower center for your topper, and starting from the end without pencil marks, make a loose coil using (C), (E), or (G). Line up the end with the last pencil mark and glue it closed.

6. PINK FLOWER

Soften the (D) strip and re-crease the folds sharply. Dip the first fold into a puddle of glue. Press that fold against one of the pencil marks on the loose coil you made for the flower's center, using a toothpick to ensure good adhesion. While the glue is wet, gently press the flower on a flat surface to make the bottoms of the two pieces flush. Match each fold up to a pencil mark, gluing each one until only two ends remain loose. Finish by gluing one end at a time.

7. GREEN FLOWER

Using the (F) strip, follow the same steps as for the pink flower, but pinch the rounded petal in the middle to make it pointy. Gently push the point toward the center of the flower to make the petals puff out and look fuller.

8. ORANGE FLOWER

Using the (H) strip, follow the same steps as for the pink flower, but pinch the rounded petal in the middle, resulting in a pointed petal. Using your tweezers, grip the petal tip and fold it left and then right, creating new creases. Open up the petal and push the tip inward to create a little "dent" in the end of each petal. Finally, gently push the two new tips toward the center of the flower to make the petals puff out and look fuller.

Step 7

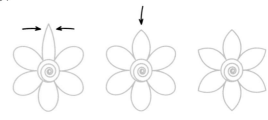

Step 8

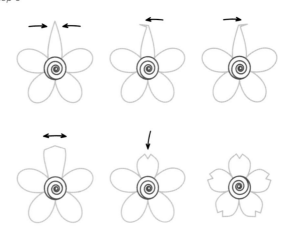

to **anna**
from **santa**

Christmas Tree Gift Tag

SKILLS YOU'LL NEED:
- V-scroll (page 12)
- Loose coil (pages 8-9)
- Same-sided scroll (page 12)
- S-scroll (page 11)
- Heart scrolls (page 12)

Project Components   SKILL LEVEL: ● ● ○ ○ ○

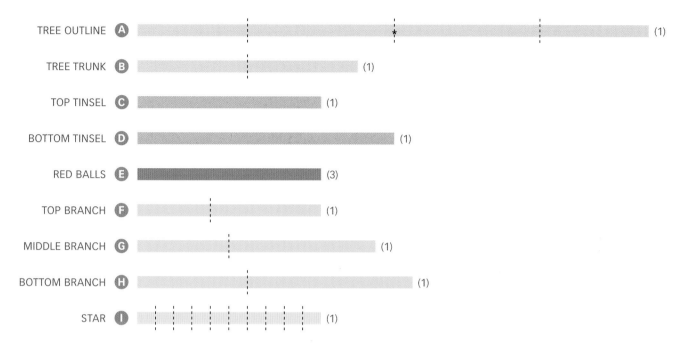

TREE OUTLINE   **A**   (1)

TREE TRUNK   **B**   (1)

TOP TINSEL   **C**   (1)

BOTTOM TINSEL   **D**   (1)

RED BALLS   **E**   (3)

TOP BRANCH   **F**   (1)

MIDDLE BRANCH   **G**   (1)

BOTTOM BRANCH   **H**   (1)

STAR   **I**   (1)

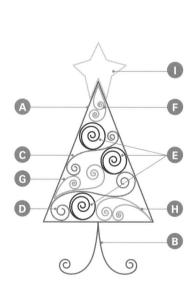

Step 2

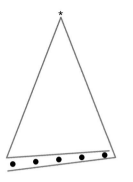

Step 3

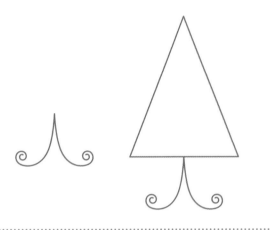

Step 4

Step 5

1. **TEMPLATE**

   Photocopy the tag on page 115 and cut it out along the outer edge.

2. **TREE OUTLINE**

   Fold strip Ⓐ into a triangle, with both ends overlapping each other to form the bottom of the tree, and then glue it closed. The asterisk (*) designates the top of the tree.

3. **TREE TRUNK**

   Create a V-scroll with the Ⓑ strip. Glue the tree outline and trunk to your gift tag.

4. **TOP AND BOTTOM TINSEL**

   Create S-scrolls with the Ⓒ and Ⓓ strips, and place them within the tree outline. Do not glue them in place yet.

5. **RED BALLS**

   Create three 7 mm loose coils using the Ⓔ strips, and place them within the tree, but do not glue them in place yet.

6. TOP, MIDDLE, AND BOTTOM BRANCHES

Create tucked heart scrolls with the Ⓕ and Ⓖ strips and a same-sided scroll with the Ⓗ strip, and nestle them in place as shown.

Adjust the elements to get them to fit. Remove one element at a time, dip it in a puddle of glue, and then place it permanently within the tree. Glue all areas where the paper touches to strengthen the design.

7. STAR

Fold the Ⓘ strip in a zig-zag pattern as shown to form a star shape, and finish your tree by gluing the star on top.

Step 6

Step 7

Framed Name

SKILLS YOU'LL NEED: • Flowers (pages 112-113) • Tight coil (page 10)

Personalized gifts have always been my favorite projects. No matter how many hours they take or how badly my neck aches, the thought is always on my mind that this person will feel special for receiving the gift, because they will see how much they mean to me. Just like love, this kind of gift is not something you can buy.

This project is not like the previous ones. The font and size shown here are just examples. The font you choose should fit the flowers from the Cupcake Toppers project and some greenery. Allow your creative side to flourish, and make your own statement in quilling!

Project Components SKILL LEVEL: ● ● ● ● ○

LETTERS **A** FONT SHOWN: ADOBE GARAMOND, 452 PT OR ABOUT ¾ INCH (1.9 CM) WIDE SO THE FLOWERS CAN FIT

FLOWERS **B** MAKE AS MANY AS NEEDED FROM CUPCAKE TOPPER, PAGE 110

STEMS - SMALL **C**

STEMS - MEDIUM **D**

STEMS - LARGE **E**

PLINTHS **F**

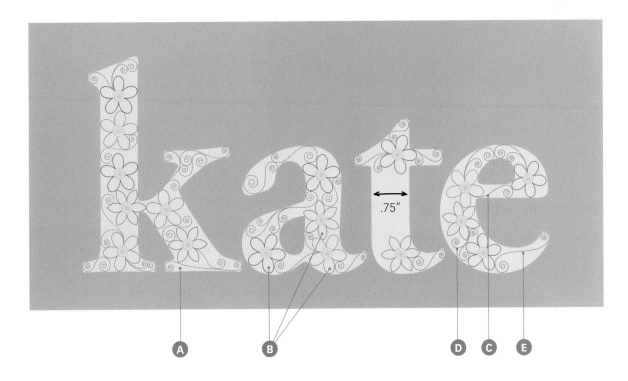

.75"

A   B   D C E

1. LETTERS

The font I used in this example is 452-point Adobe Garamond. This font has soft serifs, lending it well to quilled coils. Any font can be used, but a width of ¾ inch (1.9 cm) is ideal. It will allow the flowers to nestle comfortably.

Use a computer to print your letters in solid black onto regular printer paper. Tape or staple the sheet with your printed letters on top of your chosen cardstock. Use a craft knife or scissors to cut around the outside of your printed letters, cutting through both layers at once.

2. FLOWERS

Refer to Cupcake Toppers project (pages 112-113) for instructions on how to make the flowers. Make as many flowers as needed to fill each letter. Place the finished flowers in the largest spaces first, gluing them in place once the layout is finalized

(shown at right at 50%). Varying the spacing gives a random, unplanned appearance.

3. SMALL, MEDIUM, LARGE STEMS

Use strips Ⓒ, Ⓓ, and Ⓔ to make stems (Ⓒ = Question-mark scroll, Ⓓ = V-scrolls or same-sided scrolls, Ⓔ = S-scrolls). Fill the smaller spaces in between the flowers and amongst the serifs with the stems, varying their lengths as needed.

4. PLINTHS

Roll the Ⓕ strips into tight coils and glue them closed. Glue the dots to the back of the letters to give your monogram a raised platform and added dimension. As you can see in the illustration on the bottom of the facing page, I've used about 4–6 coils per letter.

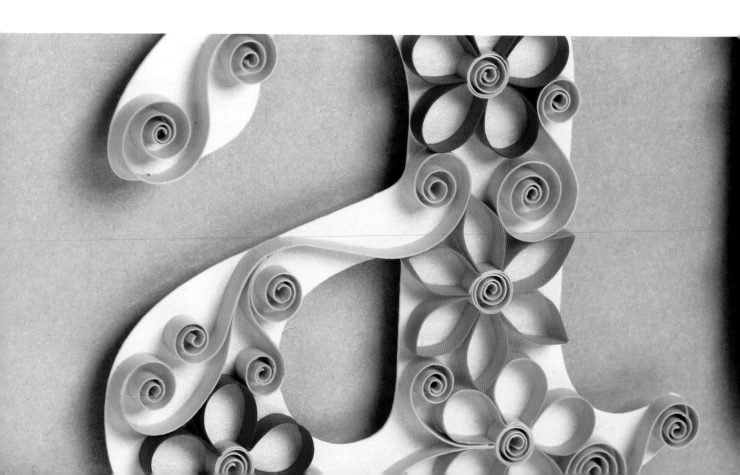

Step 2

Step 3

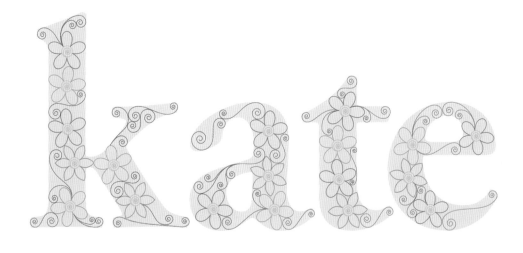

Step 4

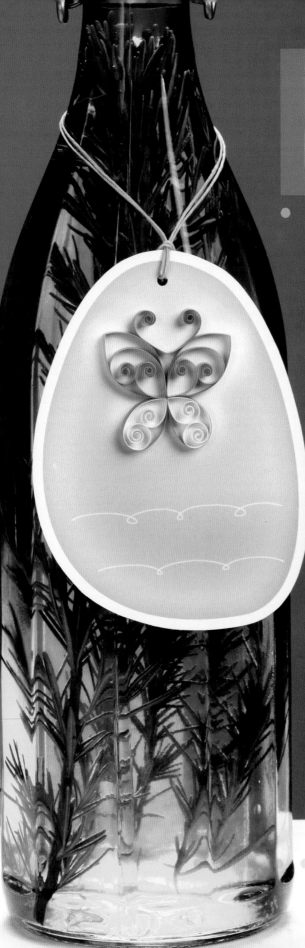

Butterfly Gift Tags

SKILLS YOU'LL NEED: • Softening (page 7)
• Asymmetric heart scrolls (page 13)
• Loose scrolls (page 10)

Project Components SKILL LEVEL: ●●○○○

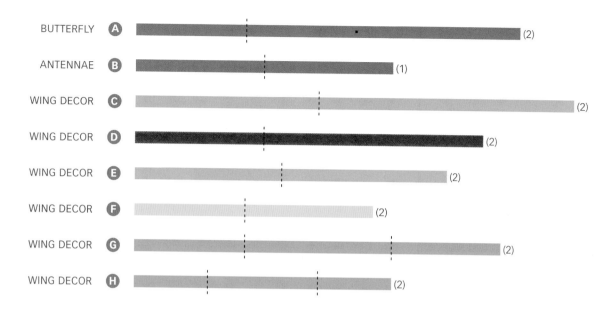

BUTTERFLY	**A**	(2)
ANTENNAE	**B**	(1)
WING DECOR	**C**	(2)
WING DECOR	**D**	(2)
WING DECOR	**E**	(2)
WING DECOR	**F**	(2)
WING DECOR	**G**	(2)
WING DECOR	**H**	(2)

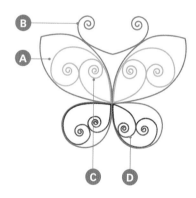

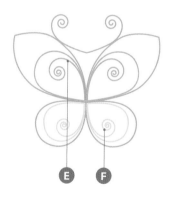

Step 1

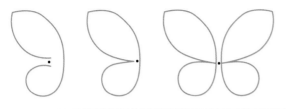

1. WING OUTLINE

These instructions are to make one set of butterfly wings. Soften both Ⓐ strips. Glue the wing ends together as shown, and then glue that seam to the pencil mark you made in the middle. Glue two together to make one butterfly. (The wings are shown at 75%)

Step 2

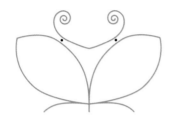

2. ANTENNAE

Create a heart scroll using the Ⓑ strip to make an antennae. Open them up and glue one to each butterfly as shown at left.

Step 3

3. 1st BUTTERFLY

Create four tucked, asymmetric heart scrolls using strips Ⓒ and Ⓓ. Place them all within the wings of one butterfly, as shown at left. Starting from the corner, dab glue in all touching areas.

4. 2nd BUTTERFLY

Soften all four Ⓔ and Ⓕ strips and fold them as indicated in the cutting guide. Create a loose scroll with the shorter segment. Wrap the longer half around the coil and glue the teardrop shape closed. Place them within the wings as shown below and glue everything together.

Step 4

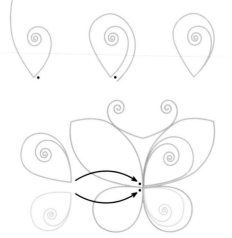

5. 3rd BUTTERFLY

Fold and soften the four Ⓖ and Ⓗ strips. Dab a small amount of glue in the folds as shown and press them together. Place the shapes into the wings. Dab glue on one side of the wing's corner and press one end in place. Repeat for the other end. Dab glue in the corner, and then push the folds into place. If needed, use pins to hold the pieces in place until the glue dries.

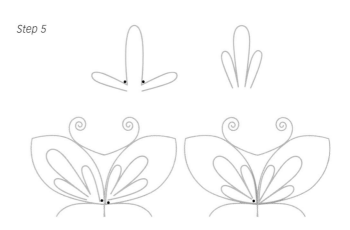

Color photocopy the tags below at 100%, and cut them out along the outlines.
Glue the butterflies within the white space provided.

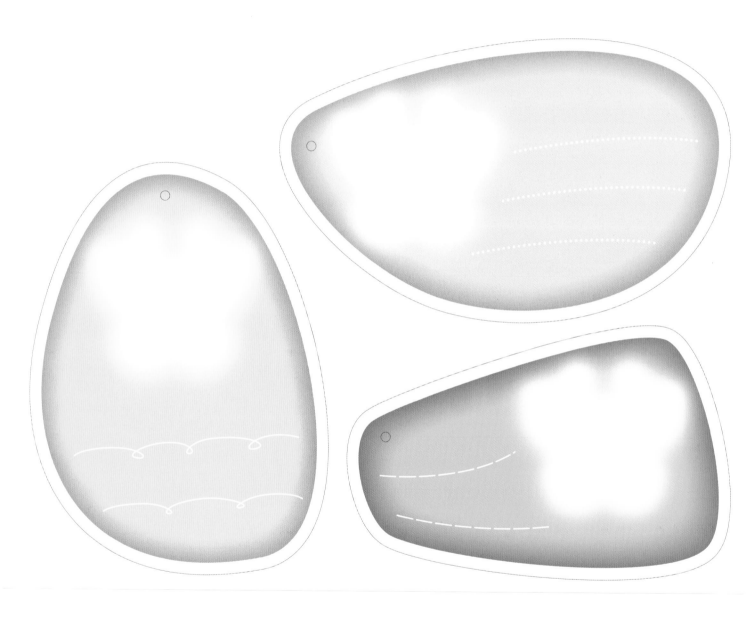

ABOUT THE AUTHOR

Cecelia Louie's love of paper began with the folding of an origami balloon at age six. She is a graduate of Emily Carr University of Art and Design in Vancouver, British Columbia, Canada. A graphic designer by day, she is a paper crafter at night.

Cecelia is a contributing author of:

- *The New Encyclopedia of Origami & Papercraft Techniques* [Running Press, 2011]

- *All Things Paper: 20 Unique Projects from Leading Paper Crafters, Artists, and Designers* [Tuttle, 2013]

To view more of her work, please visit: http://paperzen.blogspot.ca/

ACKNOWLEDGMENTS

I dedicate this book to my husband, Simon. This book exists because of your unfailing support and gentle encouragement. Your belief in me gave me the strength to keep going. You are my better half.

Thank you, Tamako, for letting me pull you into my crazy paper world and for your reassurances to "just do it and they will follow." You were essential in raising the bar for me to make a great book.

Thank you to my quilling guinea pigs, Deanne, Michelle, and Jane. Without your testing and insight, there would have been many more errors. I deeply appreciate your time and patience. I have learned so much from you all.

To my photo guru, Malcolm, thanks—I have some hair left because of your calm and logical explanations.

I'm indebted to my team at Lark for making my bucket list dream come true. Linda, your concise bird's eye view allowed me to hit the tarmac running, and your solid belief in me made me soar. Becky, I had the best time word-smithing with you. Kristi, I felt a kinship with you over all those tiny details; thank you for caring so much with me. Stewart, thank you for photographing my work in its best angles. Kerstin, my thanks to you for bringing it all together so wonderfully. Thanks for making me look so good, team!

To my family, friends, and blog readers who have oohed and aahed, I thank you for your cheerleading. The quietest clapping from the sidelines put pep in my step.

I'd like to thank my beloved parents for uprooting themselves to give me the opportunities they dreamed of in Canada. Thanks, Mom, for telling me to do whatever made me happy rather than what I thought I was supposed to be doing, for showing me how to work fast with my hands, and for being the #1 fan of anything I drew. Thanks, Dad, for instilling your unwavering work ethic and honesty in me, and for never waking me when I fell asleep in the car. Your love shows through in quiet ways, and I cherish you both, always.

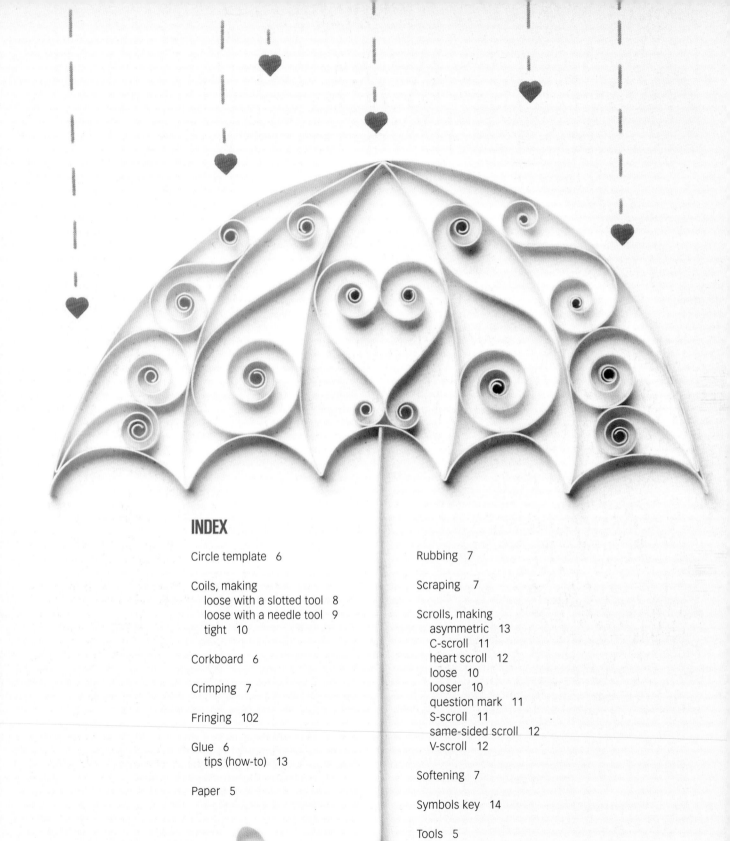

INDEX